A

River Teeth Literary Nonfiction Prize

SERIES EDITORS:
Daniel Lehman, *Ashland University*
Joe Mackall, *Ashland University*

The River Teeth Literary Nonfiction
Prize is awarded to the best work
of literary nonfiction submitted to the
annual contest sponsored by *River
Teeth: A Journal of Nonfiction Narrative.*

DOUBLE) LIFE

Discovering Motherhood

Lisa Catherine Harper

UNIVERSITY OF NEBRASKA PRESS | LINCOLN AND LONDON

Library of Congress
Cataloging-in-Publication Data
Harper, Lisa Catherine, 1966–
A double life: discovering
motherhood / Lisa Catherine Harper.
p. cm. — (River Teeth literary
nonfiction prize)
Includes bibliographical references.
ISBN 978-0-8032-3508-3 (pbk.: alk. paper)
1. Harper, Lisa Catherine, 1966–
2. Mothers—United States—
Biography. 3. Motherhood. I. Title.
HQ759.H292A3 2011
306.874'3092—dc22
[B]   2010030480

Set in Monotype Dante and Futura
by Kim Essman.
Designed by A. Shahan.

For Ella, who is not Lucy but
who is nevertheless my
light. You continue to teach
me everything about who
I am, and why.

And for Finn, who, in coming
second, is the confirmation.

Infancy conforms to nobody:
all conform to it.

RALPH WALDO EMERSON

CONTENTS

ACKNOWLEDGMENTS

I would like to thank *River Teeth Journal* first, for honoring this book with its 2010 Literary Nonfiction Prize. Every writer needs that one reader who believes passionately in her book and who has the means to bring it to print. Editors Dan Lehman and Joe Mackall gave this book that opportunity and for that I am forever grateful. Thanks are also due to Kristen Elias Rowley, Ann Baker, and the University of Nebraska Press. Chapters of this book appeared first in slightly different forms in the following online publications: "Flying Home" in *Literary Mama,* August 14, 2006 (http://literarymama.com); "Seachange" as "Remnants" in *LOST Magazine* 15 (May 2007) (http://www.lostmag.com); and "Pas de Deux" in *Switchback* 8, no. 4 (2008) (http://swback .com).

I owe my agent, Elizabeth Evans at Jean V. Naggar Literary Agency, inestimable thanks for being the first professional to believe fully in this project. Thank you for your keen and literate eye, your professional advice, and your continued support.

Thanks to all my colleagues in the MFA program at the University of San Francisco. This book would not be the same without your community, and it remains a privilege to teach with you. Specifically, Catherine Brady and Jane Anne Staw understood exactly the ways that mothering and writing are competing and complementary claims. Aaron Shurin continues to bless me with the poetry of his friendship and his lyric wisdom. Thank you for teaching me that there are many ways to enter the conversation. Lewis Buzbee has been a steady colleague, a great reader, and a superb friend. You have taught me many things—about writing, about parenting, about staying sane—that I didn't even know I needed to learn. My students at USF immerse me in the art and the rigor of nonfiction, and I am especially grateful for those students who have so gracefully made the transition to colleagues and friends. My mentors at the University of California at Davis, Joanne Feit-Diehl, Sandra M. Gilbert, Clarence Major, and David Van Leer, taught me the rigor of research, the necessity of narrative, and the experimental flight of lyric.

Jeff Gordinier has been a support and friend from the beginning of everything, and Melissa Clark made this book possible in many ways, some of which only she can understand. I'm grateful for the gift of their friendship. Many more friends and colleagues generously read early drafts of this work and offered invaluable advice (including medical expertise) including Julie Bruck, Caroline Grant, Nina Schuyler, Stephanie Barbagiovanni, and Michelle Currie Smith. Throughout my pregnancy Judith Bishop, CNM, Sharon Wiener, CNM, and Dr. Julian Parer, all at UCSF, gave generously of their expertise, intelligence, and deep commitment to mothers and infants. They confirmed my driving curiosity about exactly why this subject bears such close scrutiny by the layperson.

Tiffany Cassell looked after my children with patience, joy, and generosity so I could write. Genneal and Steve Heinzen have been the supportive in-laws and devoted grandparents every mother and child should have. My sister, Meredith Allon, and brother, Keith Harper, may not always understand my obsessions but they remain my great friends on this journey. My parents, Douglas and Patricia Harper, in their unflagging support of my work and my family and in their passionate engagement with every aspect of life, have made everything possible. My gratitude to them is inexpressible.

My deepest thanks and my fiercest love are for my children, who have lived with this book for as long as I have, and most especially for my husband, Kory Heinzen, who, with his creativity, generosity, and love, has given me the home and the marriage in which I continue to thrive, inside and out.

A DOUBLE LIFE

INSIDE)

CONCEPTION

At the end of September 2001 I traveled three thousand miles
to New Jersey to attend the wedding of my best college friend.
Somewhere over the Great Plains it dawned on me. It was a
sudden, jolting thought. Less than a thought, really, and more
like a singular moment of recognition. The sensation was like
seeing suddenly, with unmistakable clarity, the face of a long
forgotten friend, someone who had ceased to exist but who now
stood flesh and blood before me. The world dropped away, and
in silence I reckoned with the unavoidable, impossible fact.

There had been clues, of course: what I had thought was
a menstrual cycle had suddenly and inexplicably stopped. My
breasts were tender when they shouldn't have been. The previous weekend, when my husband and I had attended a weekend-
long dance festival, I had stumbled and missed my leads. I was
bone-tired, my limbs as unresponsive as a broken marionette.
Kory and I had met while dancing and our social life was an-
chored in teaching, performing, and competing in vintage swing

3

dances. It was a vital part of our marriage, but that weekend, even though scores of friends were visiting from out of town—which meant a wealth of fresh dancing partners, new tricks to learn, and old moves to show off—I could galvanize none of the energy that usually propelled me across the dance floor for hours at a time. Instead, I sat in the corner of the studio hunched against the mirror, watching with a slightly distracted longing while my husband danced with one partner after another. I was annoyed that he was dancing. I was jealous, too. But I felt too battered by fatigue to protest. Uncharacteristically, we went home early.

It was not simply that my body craved sleep, or that I was overworked, or that I had stayed up too late. I was teaching part time and went to bed early. I had my weekends and evenings to myself. It was not yet flu season. During the week after the festival, though, simple tasks, like walking to the corner store or fixing an easy dinner, proved inexplicably difficult. In the middle of this perplexing fatigue and muddle-headedness I knew that something was askew in me but for the life of me I could not imagine what.

Then, on that plane, in a single moment—really, in less time than it took to lower my tray table—the ragtag symptoms adhered and I knew. I knew that I was pregnant, and in the suspended moments that followed, other knowledge tumbled fast. I knew that my life would never return to me simply. I knew that I was frightened and perhaps crazy, for who sanely, rationally makes such a choice?

Before that day I had been vigilant about charting and tracking and monitoring my body for any markers—obvious or otherwise—of pregnancy, and I could not fathom how any woman could not know she was pregnant. But, as I discovered firsthand, the signs and symptoms of early pregnancy, which can be downright pedestrian, are easy to overlook—especially if you aren't expecting to conceive.

My own mother had been one of those women who, for many weeks, had no inkling of her pregnancy. She was a small woman, weighing ninety-five pounds on her wedding day. (Her wedding dress, with its lovely beaded ivory bodice, fit me at age thirteen and was too small by age twenty-one.) Her menstrual cycle had always been irregular and, though pregnant, she had continued to have what appeared to be a period for two months. Years later, when this biological fact surfaced in my own life, and then in the lives of several of my friends, we wondered: *Why hadn't anyone told us?* I asked my mother: "Why didn't you tell me?" She shrugged. She had forgotten. It had seemed unimportant. But this is exactly the kind of information—those seemingly minor but crucial facts—that first-time mothers crave. And it is precisely the kind of pedestrian information so easily forgotten once pregnancy and motherhood gather their unstoppable momentum.

Neither my mother nor father suspected anything when she became pregnant with me, only that she was coming down with the flu. Then one night, when she was feeling particularly worn down by the demands of her job and my father's second year of law school, my father, who believed that Snuffy's Steak House was the cure for all minor fatigues and digestive ills, proclaimed, "What you need is a good steak dinner." My mother's secretarial job provided their only income, so that dinner was a luxury. They went out on a date, a young, newly married couple like any other. But my mother couldn't eat a bite.

The next day Mom's best friend, who had her second child on the way, gently queried, "Pat, do you think you're pregnant?"

My mother, possessing an unshakeable faith in the efficacy of modern contraception, replied, "Nancy! That's impossible."

But of course it wasn't.

That morning on the plane I sat still, feeling small and invisible in my seat, stirring with private knowledge. My astonishment was not lessened by the fact that my fate was one I had chosen. The choice to become pregnant for the first time proceeds from a place of deep and willful ignorance. Yes, I had wanted a baby, but I knew nothing at all about the fate I had chosen for myself except for one visceral fact: even then I knew that I was lucky as life itself.

The next morning I woke in my childhood bed in my parents' home in New Jersey, counting the minutes until the local pharmacy opened at nine a.m. I drove through the quiet suburban streets, faced the long shelf of brightly colored boxes, and chose a test at random. Back in the quiet of the attic bathroom—which had been mine as a child and whose gently sloping walls were papered with a splashy print of bold orange and yellow flowers—I peeled the foil off the white stick, peed, and waited. A second blue line appeared in an instant, a twin to the first, a parallel being. A cry *Yes! Yes!* rose in my throat. The incontrovertible evidence stared back at me, blue on white, unmoving and unmoved. They were the simplest lines I had ever read but their certainty took my breath away. I smiled broadly. Then I smiled again. I took my time getting back down the stairs. After all the waiting, this seemed no time to rush.

When I told her, my mother cried. Then she laughed. Then she asked, redundantly, "Are you sure?" Then she hugged me. My father (not quite convinced about the reliability of the over-the-counter tests) worried about false positives. Distracted by the drama unfolding in my belly, I ignored them both. "Yes," I said quietly, "I'm sure."

Later that morning, as soon as I thought the time difference allowed, I called my husband, but there was no answer. I found him already at work and told him the news. He was characteristically subdued. "That's so cool," he said. But I heard a thrill in his voice and the catch between what he said and what he wouldn't say because he was at work, surrounded by colleagues. Somehow the news felt secret, not yet ours to share widely. It collapsed the distance between us, and we inhabited one mind, one moment of suspended uncertainty.

My husband is an artist, so he has always trafficked in images rather than words. It is in his nature to be elliptical and reserved. Always he will tend to keep things to himself, sometimes for better, sometimes for worse. On the one hand, this innate privacy makes for a profound source of discretion. I can count on him not to be hyperbolic, and he can maintain the kind of even keel that I've struggled to find all my life. He is the voice of reason and stability in our home. On the other hand, this reserve can occasion a breakdown of communication, a terseness that borders on rudeness, and a lack of sentiment that has made me call him, on rare, indignant occasions, emotionally crippled. That morning, in his quiet joy, I knew exactly why I loved him. Beyond this first fact there was everything and nothing. A wordless intimacy settled between us, then we hung up the phone and got on with the day.

Later that night we spoke again, and he confessed, "I had a grin on my face all day. And I kept tearing up and wanting to tell everyone." I lay in my parents' den, covered against the autumn chill by an old blanket, and I spoke quietly. We talked about the fact and around the fact, and said a whole lot of nothings and repeated ourselves some more. But the news of conception had shocked him outside of himself. That was how I knew. That was how I knew that the baby beginning inside of me would transform everything I knew, not just about myself but also about my husband, our marriage, our life together. In fact, everything I knew about the world and my place in it was about to be reconceived.

EXPECTING

The story of motherhood doesn't really begin, at least not always, with the fact of conception. Ask anyone who has found her life transformed by a baby and she will tell you about the time *before*—the moment, days, weeks, months, or even years— when she waited. Sometimes, of course, as in my mother's case, a pregnancy takes you by surprise so that one day you find yourself suddenly, unexpectedly pregnant. But for very many others, there is first the decision—the Yes! Sure! Why not? Let's have a baby!—and then the inevitable wait. Some couples make this decision easily; children are what they've always wanted. Others make the choice only after long reflection and deliberation. Our friends, for instance, came to it after nearly ten years of marriage. But once that decision is made, there's a gap. Some will tell you they got pregnant immediately. Others will tell you long stories about agonizing years of infertility treatments. Every story is different, but the waiting is not. All parents experience that interregnum, a time between two rulers, a time when the solo life seems less sovereign but the dictatorship of the child is not yet an established fact. For many women, it can be a chaotic, unsettling time: we're not pregnant, which is the one thing we long to be. It makes a lot of us irrational—crazed with the desire for the thing that seems obtainable but which remains always out of reach—until that shock of a day when it isn't. This time of waiting is a pause, a hiccup, a disjunction in your life when you're trying to get ready, and you think you are ready, but there's nothing yet to be ready for.

For me the interregnum had begun months before, on a foggy morning at the tail end of June. That day I stood alone in my flannel pajamas and slippers on the cold tiles of our bathroom floor. Facing the mirror but carefully avoiding the bleary, rumpled image of my unshowered reflection, I ritualistically punched a pill through the foil of the dial pak. Kory had gone to work hours before, and aside from the occasional pounding footsteps of our landlady above, our small San Francisco apartment was silent. I second-guessed my decision one final time then went ahead with it. I flushed the first pill of my new cycle down the toilet. Why I bothered to flush that tiny green pill rather than simply throw away the whole card is not easily explained, but it has something to do with deliberation and ceremony. I was an academic and a writer. It was my job to think things through. Of course, I was also making certain that I wouldn't change my mind later that day, fish the pack out of the trash can, and continue on with my happy, unpregnant life.

Twenty-four hours later, life was simpler. Wake, pee, drink coffee, brush teeth, *don't take pill*, shower, apply makeup, *don't take pill*, dress, dry hair. *Don't remember to take pill.* All day long I thought *no pill. No pill*, I chanted to myself. It was a simple thing, really, a small omission, one less remembering to clutter my mind. And yet, that singular forgetting freed a space as vast as the pill was small, as undefined as the pill was precise.

The following Saturday, my husband and I lay in our bed in

the lazy, sexy, unencumbered way that only childless couples have. We were deciding, if such lethargy can really be likened to any active process of decision, when we might want to get up, brew coffee, make our way over to the farmers market. We had spent another late Friday night at the local club where our friends and our vintage dance troop gathered regularly to dance the Lindy Hop to a six-piece jump blues band that had resurrected, with astonishing intensity, the ecstatic, infectious sound of small-group bands like Louis Jordan, Roy Milton, and Louis Prima. They were the band of choice for serious dancers, and the musicians were good friends of ours. They'd played at our wedding, and in those days we saw them at least twice a week.

We had been at the Hi-Ball Lounge, a small, dark bar that fused San Francisco hipster cool with Vegas lounge (the décor was upholstered zebra print wallpaper running the length of one long wall and tiny tables snuggled up to the wine-colored bench). We'd grabbed a booth up front, near the band, then piled our wool Pendletons, belt-backs, and San Francisco Jitterbug jackets in the corner, set down a few drinks, and spent the rest of the night dancing with boyfriends, husbands, partners, and each other. We did group dances like the Shim Sham, outdid each other in jam circles with new tricks, faster footwork, even aerials that sometimes tossed the girl dangerously close to either the stage or the onlookers. We traded dance partners all night long. It was crowded and sometimes a little frenetic on the tiny dance floor, but Kory and I rarely sat down, except during band breaks. We had met in a dance club in Los Angeles, and our early romance had been fueled by dancing. Mostly, we behaved like addicts. Our first dates took place at dances and workshops. We shared old movie clips, learned new steps, taught ourselves tricks, and acquired a wide circle of friends. We spent long hours discovering bands and new (old) music, searched through racks of vintage clothes, and choreographed performance routines or jam circle sequences. It was a heady time, and the early thrill of physical attraction was doubled by the physical intensity of the dance. Lindy Hop is challenging to master and exhilarating to dance. But as complicated as the dance is to execute, its pleasures are simple. Kory and I could toss on vintage threads and spend several hours throwing ourselves around the dance floor like a couple of teenagers. After years of ballet and modern dance training, what I loved most about the Lindy Hop was its unscripted, spontaneous nature. Out on the dance floor you never knew what might happen. Very soon I realized that dancing with Kory made me happy. He was fit and athletic, with a strong jaw and a clean-cut style. He had dark hair, green eyes, and really straight teeth. His sense of humor equaled his sense of music. I found it hard not to smile when I was Lindy Hopping, and it was impossible not to feel my anxiety evaporate when Chick Webb was drumming. As time went on I realized that Kory made me happy, too. It was this happiness—so straightforward and simple and, frankly, old-fashioned—that was a revelation for me. Being with Kory, like dancing, was an easy, uncomplicated pleasure. Soon I was hooked on both.

That Saturday morning, like so many that had come before, we were tired and a little hungry, but perfectly content. Light streamed through the single bay window behind us. We were warm and comfortable and our mood was as bright as the day that faced us. Kory turned to me and joked, "Are you ovulating?" I found this funny, and then sexy, which I took as a sign of just how much our marriage had changed me.

When we made love we were awake and sober and the room was bright with day. We knew exactly what we were doing. The morning rose around us, and we held each other as we had so many times before. But now my husband seemed a revelation. Dancing had taught us how to do many things together; things that made us laugh and things that made us fight; things that surprised us; things fueled by music and muscle and sheer joy; things with our feet, things that spun, things on the ground; even things up in the air. But stretched alongside Kory that morning—our limbs, torso, arms entwined—I loved something new about him. I loved the risk he had agreed to take as much as I loved the long, vulnerable expanse of his skin. Making love that morning was not wholly unlike the complicated give-and-take between a lead and follow, where the dancers have a plan but everything changes in the moment, when you respond to the music but also to each other. That morning we didn't know what would happen after we made love, and this mystery ushered in a new kind of intimacy, the same kind of intense mindfulness of each other and of the moment that we had when we danced. Suddenly, sex was more than pleasure, and as this pleasure raced toward meaning, it left in its wake the knowledge that this was, in its most base, Darwinian sense, what sex was meant for. That thing I had been most afraid of for most of my life—becoming pregnant, having a child—was suddenly the thing I wanted most. Everything old seemed new again.

After, we rose slowly and showered and went to the farmers market, where we shopped and ate a late breakfast. I did not get pregnant that morning, but it was, in many ways, the day we began to wait.

For fifteen years I had determined to control my body and my reproductive destiny. It was partly politics—the phrase we all had on our lips—but it was more than that, too. I was stalked by fear of pregnancy, HIV/AIDS, other, less deadly but still deeply inconvenient STDs. To ward off my anxieties I employed at least one form of birth control, sometimes two, and, on special occasions, three. No matter what the trouble, no inconvenience could be spared against the lurking fear of getting pregnant. In fact, I can remember when pregnancy and disease seemed nearly equivalent threats. Back then, before Kory, a child was not a child. A child was something that would take over my body and drag my life into darkness and disarray.

"Other people have done it," my college boyfriend argued, when we confronted a potential failure of birth control.

"Not me," I said. "Not me and not now."

"It might not be so bad. I could get a job."

"Maybe not ever," I said.

I knew intuitively that a child would turn my life inside out, that having a baby would irrevocably change everything about me, and that I was in no way up to the task. The day the pregnancy test came back negative I went on the pill, a decision that was also, ironically, fueled by the cautionary tale that was my own life. Several years prior, in a well-intentioned but logic-confounding admission, my mother had informed me that I had been "a mistake."

Kory and I, on the other hand, had moved slowly toward our decision. For a year we let the idea rise and set between us. Every few months after our wedding I pestered him, "Do you want to have a baby? What do you think about having a baby?" "Okay," he would reply calmly. "I would like that." A few days later I would ask again, "Are you ready?" "Sure," he would say, shrugging and smiling. "Why not?"

I did and didn't believe him. On the one hand he is six years my junior. When we first met, I connived a glance at his driver's license in order to ensure that he was, in fact, old enough to drink. If I didn't feel quite grown up enough to have a baby, how in the world could he? While he'd held a stable job for years, he didn't exactly look the part of a grownup. In fact, he didn't look like any father I had ever known. The fact that his job as a visual development artist, first for video games and then for feature films, had never required him to wear business attire, that he was surrounded all day by like-minded, pop-culture savvy young men (and a few women) did nothing to convince me that we were ready to meet the demands of parenthood. I had been a graduate student for half a decade when we met, and while my solitary writing life merged nicely with his solitary artist's life, we were hardly the prime candidates for parenthood that I knew some young couples—with steady incomes, homes of their own, large retirement accounts—to be.

But, in fact, Kory was ready. He had a clearer, easier sense of his future than I did. He had a sense of humor. He liked stability and the fact that we were building a life together. He saw nothing wrong with moving to the suburbs. He was as quietly confident about having a baby as he was about other important things in his life. This, of course, was another one of the reasons I married him.

In the end, the year of questions was a year for my benefit. I wasn't sure that I wanted a baby. What would a baby mean for us, for me? I had no idea, and I knew of no way to imagine the prospects. But after months of living with the idea, of bringing it out into the light, shaking it around, and making it live between us for a few moments at a time, after simply asking over and over, *Are you ready? Am I ready?* The idea began to appeal to me. Our one-year anniversary rolled around, and, for the first time in my life, I wanted a child.

That June we entered a liminal time, the time of trying and waiting and waiting and trying. My younger sister, Meredith, already the mother of two girls, was nearly as excited as I was but vastly more practical. I called her at least twice a week with absurd and arcane questions that no one could have possibly answered. To her credit, she answered patiently.

"When should I expect to ovulate?"

"I don't know."

"How often should we try?"

"As much as you can."

"When do I have to stop drinking wine?"

"Probably now."

"Can I eat shellfish?"

"Of course."

"Do you like the name Everett?" (Our grandfather's name.)

"Some names are not meant for children."

Most often she counseled, "Don't think too much," which was, of course, impossible advice to follow.

Contrary to popular opinion and your mother's admonitions, it is not that easy to get pregnant. Only about one in five healthy young couples that engage in intercourse around the time of ovulation will conceive. On average, a woman in her twenties will take four and half months to conceive, a woman in her late thirties, ten to twelve months. If you are under thirty most infertility specialists will not grant you an appointment until you have been actively trying for a full year, although any woman over thirty who is anxious about becoming pregnant should see a doctor who treats infertility. Of the more than 200 million sperm that are deposited into the vagina during intercourse, only about 100 or 200 will cross the cervix and reach the vicinity of the egg. Once fertilization has occurred, the egg and sperm must be healthy, with the right number of chromosomes; the zygote must become a blastocyst and lodge properly in the uterus. But up to half of all zygotes never become blastocysts, and only about 70 to 75 percent of all blastocysts properly implant in the uterus. Just over half of these survive past two weeks, and, even then, 16 percent are spontaneously aborted. Doctors estimate that the actual rate of miscarriage before a pregnancy is positively diagnosed may be as high as 20 to 40 percent. This means that many, many women, unawares, have likely experienced a miscarriage at some point in their lives. Compound this figure with the lowered fertility rates that can be caused by fairly common conditions like stress, sleeplessness, smoking, and diabetes, and it is easy to see why fertilization is not exactly a given.

I had been on birth control for more than a decade and

couldn't remember what a regular period was like. Very quickly, the pregnancy that had seemed inevitable to me now seemed quite evitable. Even, on some days, impossible.

To help pinpoint my ovulation date I bought a basal thermometer. I had read about these highly precise, digital instruments somewhere and had a vague recollection of the concept from our mandatory Catholic pre-marriage retreat, so I promptly trotted over to the local pharmacy and found one, which I stashed in the slim drawer of my bedside table. I reasoned to my sister, who thought I was overdoing it, how did I know I was ovulating at all, much less with any regularity?

Basal body temperature is the temperature of the body at rest. For the first two weeks of a woman's menstrual cycle the influence of estrogen tends to keep this temperature low, around 97 to 97.5 degrees Fahrenheit. Upon ovulation, this temperature will sometimes drop significantly. Then the release of progesterone, which follows ovulation, will cause it to rise by as much as .5 or .9 degrees, and it will remain elevated until menstruation begins. A woman trying to conceive can learn three things by charting her basal body temperature: at what time in her cycle she tends ovulate, whether her cycles are regular, and whether the second phase of the menstrual cycle (the luteal phase) is significantly long (at least ten days from ovulation to menstruation) to allow for implantation. A basal temperature chart cannot predict ovulation—indeed, people most dedicated to "natural" family planning espouse diligent and constant monitoring of cervical mucus and cervical position along with basal body temperature—but it can certainly indicate irregularities and offer a good overview of the menstrual cycle. So while in theory it's a relatively simple thing, in reality it's anything but easy to chart with exactitude. Basal body temperature must be measured immediately upon waking, before any physical activity and preferably at the same time each morning, with a thermometer precise to the tenth of a degree. You must have had at least three hours of uninterrupted sleep, and illness or alcohol consumption can affect the measurement, as can divergence from the appointed waking hour, since basal body temperature tends to rise by .2 degrees or more with each half hour increment. In my obsession to become pregnant none of this seemed especially onerous. In fact, it seemed like a very reasonable approach to the situation. My mother and sister thought otherwise, and bluntly told me so.

Every morning, as Kory's alarm went off, before I even opened my eyes, I rolled over and reached for the lavender thermometer. I lay warm under the covers, listening to the stick's slow beep, opening my eyes only when the final triple beep signaled that my temperature had registered. I duly marked the number on the columned chart and went back to sleep.

After two months I had a clear, pretty arc. On day thirteen my temperature spiked with an unmistakable, precise jump of .5 degrees Fahrenheit. I imagined the egg popping through its ovarian casing, being swept into the Fallopian tubes, floating, and waiting, waiting, waiting.

I waited anxiously, too, for I would not, after all, be a young mother. At six months past thirty-five I was at that age when rates for conception fall, rates for postnatal complications rise, and rates for Down syndrome and other birth defects increase. I scoured health books, pregnancy books, the Internet for information. I quoted statistics to reassure or to confirm my worst fears. Colleagues on fertility drugs and friends who had adopted were familiar facts. I knew two women in one office with twins, at least one the result of fertility treatments. Most days I wondered: Would I be one of those women unable to get pregnant?

Other days I convinced myself that my darkest fears were premature. I was healthy and fit and my family history, as my sister reminded me, was not only very clean but also very fertile. While these facts had no real medical bearing on the risks and possibilities for my own pregnancy, they nevertheless reassured me. I reminded myself of the women who continued to conceive and bear healthy children after thirty. My sister and best friend were eager to offer these kinds of anecdotes: friends, friends of friends, cousins, someone my friend swore had sex only once, an ex-boyfriend's wife, a college roommate who had recently had twins, a college friend, a casual acquaintance, all those celebrities. When I considered the statistics it amazed me that anyone ever got pregnant. When I heard the anecdotal evidence I wondered that anyone didn't.

This raised another issue: everyone seemed to be pregnant before me. Everywhere I went I found new babies and glowing, pregnant mothers. I was gripped by irrational envy and sometimes by the deep fear that the job of motherhood would never be mine. Having reached the point in my life where I was finally eager to have a child, I wished we had conceived yesterday. I wished that we already had a child. Or two. Or, on especially bad days, three. I read my alumni magazine with chagrin. One afternoon, after reading a blurb about two classmates who had just welcomed their second child, I expressed my irrational, uncharitable jealousy to my husband. I was angrily straightening up the part of the living room that doubled as our dining room but which also collected all manner of my papers. As my husband carefully put clean dishes into our hutch, he chided me, "Be rational. We just started trying."

"They're both M.D.-Ph.D.s," I pointed out.

"You're a Ph.D.," he responded, quite accurately.

"They probably live in a mansion and their children are brilliant." I gestured with a pile of loose papers around our small, two-bedroom flat.

"They live in the Midwest," he said. "Our rent is probably higher than their mortgage."

I sighed and shut up. I was not appeased, but I tried to follow Kory's lead. I resolved to wait and do the right things. I exercised more. I tried to get enough sleep. I bought organic food. Even Kory was only half-joking when he talked about protecting the health of his not-yet-conceived child. When I asked for a sip of his wine one night at dinner he said, "A sip for you is like thirty keggers for those fifteen cells." I scowled at him and took that sip anyway. But, also, I went to church. I prayed.

Ultimately, I was surprised by the effortlessness of it. Three months collapsed, and the period of waiting evaporated, as if it had never existed at all. I was not pregnant and then I was, and in that exchange of breath my life was irreparably divided. All pregnancy narratives have this epiphany—the moment when the pregnant woman thinks: What the hell was I thinking? For a minute I stood in the kitchen of my mother's house and wondered, like many other first-time mothers must wonder, if it had happened too fast. I replayed all the familiar clichés: we should have bought a house, should have saved more (some, any) money, should have finished (fill in the appropriate long-term project here), should have found a (new, any) job. But this was a decision of the heart, not the mind, and, in any case, the deed was done and there was nothing to be done about it. We would be carried along by the new story, whatever it would be.

Slowly, that indeterminate, elusive state of expecting began to assume meaning. What would I look like in eight months? What would my child look like? What size would it be? What gender? Would it paint precociously like its father? Love books like its mother? Would it inherit its father's talent for soccer? Its mother's inability to sing?

This expectation was different from any I had known before. It was different from being ten and longing for that royal blue satin baseball jacket, or from being in the thick of graduate school and striving to pass my oral exams, or anticipating writing the last word of my dissertation. It was different from imagining my first job or planning our first trip to the French Laundry or even my first visit to Kory in Los Angeles when we were dating. The preparation would be nothing like the training we endured for the U.S. Open competition. It was even different from waiting for the proposal, then the marriage, that had brought us to this juncture in the first place.

For all of those things, I had at least some context. But having a baby confounded my imagination. One night, after I had returned from New Jersey, Kory switched off the TV and turned to me. "I'm excited about what will happen," he said, "but I don't want to be too excited to enjoy everything happening right now." He held me and I looked at him quizzically. What was happening right now? I supposed he meant the pregnancy, the getting ready, our last few months together as a child-free couple. I curled in close to him and agreed. "I know," I said. "I'm trying." Beyond the bedroom the rest of the apartment was dark. I found it much easier to worry about the future, to make plans or anticipate or study up or simply ignore what was happening.

Kory was right. It was this kind of wisdom, his ability to find joy in the dailiness of life, that had convinced me to marry him. There would be time for plans. So for the first time in my life I found myself rooted in the present, fully mindful of the life I was living. I knew I could look ahead and try to imagine what I could not even begin to comprehend. But I also knew that all my imaginings of pregnancy, childbirth, and the long years of motherhood would most certainly be wrong. The worries I had now were sure to be misplaced, and the ones that I ought to have had could not possibly have occurred to me then. Who would benefit if I worried my mind smooth like so many beads?

Slowly, the anticipation and anxiety that had ruled my life for as long as I could remember began to dissipate. There were not so many days left for us to be alone together. I was happy being pregnant and happy with my husband. I thought I ought to enjoy these things before they vanished, mark them both while I had the time and the mind to attend to them. There was a great change taking hold of my body and somehow it had taken hold of my mind, too, and it cautioned me: *Slow down!*

Motherhood meant change. That was its bedrock. That was the difficulty to be embraced. If I could understand this change, if I could make my peace with it, then maybe someday I would measure up and become a mother. In the beginning I had no idea how this would transpire.

I knew one thing: expecting meant not expecting. I couldn't worry about how a child might turn out, or how I would rise (or not) to the occasion. Our job was simply to love and in that loving to let go of fear. In small increments I began to live on the edge of hope, to hover there in something akin to delight, fully conscious of danger and failure but equally determined not to gaze too long into that darkness.

SOMETHING
FROM NOTHING

The fall I became pregnant there seemed to be darkness every-where. On the day that our daughter was conceived, we woke in the dark predawn and made love, oblivious that three thousand miles away passenger jets had been flown murderously into the towers of the World Trade Center. My husband went to work. I went back to sleep, warm and hopeful.

A few hours later I was awakened by my mother's voice on the answering machine: "A terrible disaster . . . your father . . ." I ran to the phone. She told me the news.

It had happened hours before. The towers had collapsed, and what I saw when I saw was the New York skyline engulfed in smoke, altered irrevocably. As I stared and stared, dumbstruck, at that iconic site from my childhood, I could not wrap my mind around the annihilation. What was dependable had failed, what had seemed indispensable was not. The towers smoldered like extinguished candles, and despair sank deep within me as I watched their collapse, over and over again. In that expanse of death, in what those images could *not* reveal, everything else was eclipsed. The apocalypse of images was uncanny in the truest sense, *unheimlich,* un-homelike. The unfamiliar in the midst of the familiar. Like a chant or a dirge, I recalled the final chilling line of Wallace Stevens's "The Snow Man": "Nothing that is not there and the nothing that is."

Although the San Francisco morning was bright, the world was suddenly dark. I worried about my father's short trip home from the city of Newark to the New Jersey suburbs. I worried about my friends in Manhattan. I worried about my husband on his way to work and my friends crossing the Bay Area bridges. I worried about my brother-in-law, who travels too much, and my sister, who lives not far from Chicago. I wanted my husband home, where I could touch him.

I called my friends in New York, my sister, my friends who traveled in the Bay Area, my husband's work, where he had not yet arrived. I was lucky. My family and friends were safe. It was not until two days later that I learned that a high school classmate of my sister, a grammar school classmate of mine, and one of my brother's best friends had died that day. They left behind worlds of ordinary love and extraordinary grief, a fiancée, two wives, and five small children.

My husband, having seen the news in the coffee shop, never made it to work. Later that morning we sat in silence in the living room, side by side on our new couch, riveted by the television, as if the repetition of images might pave some rocky path to understanding: Why? And, How? I think we both hoped that watching, over and over, might provide closure. Of course there would be none of that. Mayor Giuliani, when asked to describe the scene, said simply, "I don't know that I really can describe it." And, again, "I don't think anything went through my mind." It seemed an appropriate response. Words failed on that day, but without the proper language—and there could be none—there was no way of explaining what it was we were seeing. We were like the man, blind from birth, who is suddenly restored to sight and awakens to a world he can see but cannot comprehend. There would be no comprehension, no closure, no sense to this narrative. Only the slow revolutions of change, grief, fear.

In the early afternoon we walked to the ocean. Since we lived at the far western edge of the city, where a long line of pastel-colored houses stretched along the coast, this was something we did daily, out of habit and out of need. We loved the beach even when the water was too cold and the current too dangerous to swim in. Only the most bracing wind could keep us away. It didn't matter if the weather was warm and the skies clear, or if the clouds were a single sheet of gunmetal gray, or if the ocean was casting off a spray of mist or a damp blanket of fog. That afternoon it was inevitable that we would leave our flat and wordlessly turn west.

The day was beautiful and clear, an exceedingly rare thing in that part of San Francisco, and since businesses and schools had closed, Sunset Beach was full of people. Families and young children, pairs of friends, couples, solitary walkers were scattered across the sand. It was windless; the dune grasses were still and the sand was warm. Children wore shorts or rolled up their pants. Some of them waded in the surf. The normally busy Great Highway ran the length of the beach behind the dunes, but today there were very few cars. In spite of the crowd, the beach was silent. We seemed suspended in time, not frozen, exactly, but painfully present in each moment. Above us the vast expanse of blue offered no shelter, and its brightness felt ominous. We walked farther down our stretch of beach than we ever had, talking, then not talking. There, at the edge of the country, it was easy to imagine the end of the world.

Back home, Kory turned on the TV, but I could no longer watch. For the rest of the afternoon I stood at the kitchen table mixing eggs and flour in a rhythmic circle, gathering the dough into small round balls. In the background the news was insistent. Arms dusted in flour, I kneaded and rolled and cut. I fed the smooth, elastic dough through the steel machine. Over and over, through the rollers like a mantra, the pasta stretched and lengthened into cool, yellow sheets. It grew strong and supple. I covered the table with those sheets and cut *capellini, linguini, pappardelle*. Some I dried, some I froze, some we would eat fresh for dinner. Even as I let the work soothe the edges of my grief, I felt guilty knowing there were many who would be too grieved to eat tonight, or tomorrow, or for many days to come.

Later, when it was nearly dusk, we went to bed. Neither of us had much heart for making love, but it was also all we had heart for. And so, on the most tragic day we had known, we lit a candle and made love again. We made love because we could, because it was one of the few strengths left to us. We made love because I felt my husband's life might be snatched from me at any moment. We made love because the bed felt safe and our bodies, real and warm and alive, shocked us into love. We made love because we had been lucky and were fortunate enough to understand this. We made love because we needed to feel a little bit brave. Just once, I turned to Kory and spoke. "Do we really want to bring a child into this world?"

Without pausing, he answered, "Maybe it will help make the world a better place."

In our own small way we affirmed ourselves against all that death. The smallness of our act, the futility of it, the great irony of it: none of this was lost on me. But these small assertions of self, of love, these are the only powers that most of us have.

For days we watched as the full reach of horror revealed itself. For days I woke consumed with grief, aware of pain before I was aware of its origin. I cried in the shower, on walks along the beach, after lunch, anytime my mind became too quiet. All the while I wondered, *Am I pregnant? What if I am pregnant?* To have life emerge out of such death, to bear a child who chased so closely on death's heels barely seemed possible. It seemed a bold and defiant act. I thought if I were to have a girl I would name her after my father's mother, Lucy: *lux*, light.

While in this state I mustered the courage to board that plane where the baby announced itself. At the wedding we celebrated aboard a rustic barge docked in Red Hook. To the north of us, the southern tip of Manhattan glowed in the sunset. So close as to make the distance seem swimmable, the Statue of Liberty rose from Ellis Island. Our vision was altered, the view different than it had been for many, many years, and as we waited for the ceremony to begin we silently took note of this, then turned our sights inward.

The barge was crowded and warm and filled with many old friends, most of them New Yorkers, all of them still shaken and somber. All of them had stories. One had witnessed the devastation from her apartment as she fed her baby breakfast. A new father had lost his father-in-law. Many others—including the bride—had lost friends, coworkers, acquaintances. The rehearsal dinner had been moved at the last minute because it was planned to have been celebrated in the restaurant at the top of the towers.

I told only my two closest friends what I had discovered on the plane and confirmed that morning. The fact seemed both irrelevant and irreverent to the larger facts of the night. I wandered the party, greeted at every table by old friends. Yet I felt myself a stranger. Who was I, now that I was pregnant? Who would I become? I was doubly displaced: haunted both by what was inside me and what was outside, too. It seemed that I had disappeared right along with the world I thought I knew.

As the evening wore on, the solemnity of the ceremony and the seriousness of the time softened a little, as we understood our obligation to celebrate as much as to remember and mourn.

After all, we loved the bride and groom, and our job was to usher them into their new life with hope. A jug band, a red velvet cake, and (for everyone else) many drinks later we had not forgotten what was out there, beyond the boat, but neither had we forgotten the life that rose up inside. We understood the wisdom of the lines by Czeslaw Milosz, which my friend had read after her vows, completely and finally aware that we must "watch what is, though it fades away." It was coincidence that I found myself pregnant when I did, a kind of perfect storm of circumstance. But it was still true that both events, the public and the private, conspired to effect a similar change. I was to take note of the here and now. I was to understand acutely my place in the world. Filled by my own new love and by my love for my friend and her husband, surrounded by the chaos of friendship and grief, all at once I was both inside and outside myself—which was exactly the point.

SIGNS AND SYMPTOMS

By the sixth week I was sick. Week after slow week, the nausea refused to abate. I woke nauseated, was dogged by nausea all day, went to bed nauseous. Standing, I was sick; sitting, I was sick; lying on my side, I was sick. I was sick writing; I was sick reading; I was sick teaching. Although I vomited only twice, I felt possessed, as if I had fallen down a rabbit hole into a wonderland of fatigue and illness. The pressure of it was immense and not unlike grief in its relentless, tidal churning. I felt lost, not simply distracted and unmoored as the victim of an accident might be, but truly befogged. I was not what I had been, but instead something possessed, slower, weaker, and much, much dumber. Vomiting, at least, would have provided some reprieve, a rare moment of clarity, but I was so sick that not even a sliver of the self I had been remained.

One lunch, I sat at the kitchen table facing a small white plate on which I had placed a ring of saltine crackers and a slice of white cheddar cheese. I forced myself to take one small bite. I chewed, swallowed, and fought the bile that rose in my throat. I took a breath, another bite. I had not thought it possible to eat so slowly. Half an hour later, three crackers were gone and lunch was over.

Ironically, eating, the one thing that could stave off the nausea, was the same thing that intensified it. A smell, any distinct smell, made me lunge for a clean kitchen towel, a blanket, a pillow to cover my face and smother my senses. The espresso machine was banished from the kitchen. Anything fried, stewed, or roasted was out of the question. I ate hard-boiled egg whites, plain macaroni noodles. At lucky moments I could manage a peanut butter sandwich on soft white bread, but never a sliver of crust, which I removed with the precision of a Japanese housewife. I stopped cooking altogether. I learned to keep certain foods instantly accessible so as to take advantage of those momentary respites, slim windows of time when the nausea miraculously, inexplicably abated. I stockpiled vanilla yogurt, kept a sleeve of saltines in the car, filled the pantry with so-called energy bars. I sipped canned chicken broth, snuck single spoons of vanilla ice cream, and recharged at random hours of the night on monochromatic bowls of Life cereal. Stacks of unread cooking magazines grew on the kitchen table.

Before the pregnancy I had regularly begun musing about dinner once breakfast was finished. Now the mere thought of food turned my stomach. Gone were the leisurely dinners, the search for new restaurants, my furtive cookbook reading and recipe board–searching. I could no longer plan a meal or shop for groceries, nor even spend a long Saturday morning with Kory lingering at the farmers market until lunch. While I focused all of my effort on managing the turmoil that churned in my gut, Kory looked on, rather helplessly, as bewildered by my body as I was. In fact, my sickness forged new territory for both of us. I was no longer the partner that I had been, and many of the routines of our life were disrupted in the early weeks. My inability to eat, to cook, to feed myself and my husband, to walk any farther than the distance from couch to bed, even to converse after work like a normal person: these were the first indications of the enormous changes that motherhood would wreak upon my body and, ultimately, on our marriage. "Morning" sickness (*If only*, I often thought) was our early warning signal, had we known enough to heed its message.

Of course, my experience was perfectly normal. Nausea and vomiting in pregnancy are as common as flies at an August picnic. Up to 85 percent of all pregnant women in Western cultures experience some form of nausea or vomiting, and while the symptoms tend to be most intense in the mornings, they are not circumscribed by the diurnal clock. Symptoms may appear around week six, as they did in my case, and may disappear by week twelve (thus the common association of morning sickness with the first trimester). But they may emerge as early as week two and, in rare cases, continue throughout pregnancy. During her first pregnancy my sister vomited all day and went to bed at six o'clock. She lost thirteen pounds in her first trimester. Though undiagnosed at the time, she seems to have been a victim of a specific and relatively rare condition known as *hyperemesis gravidarum*, which is "excess vomiting in the pregnant state." My mother experienced a similarly severe sickness during her first pregnancy. By the time she knew the accident that was me was on the way, my mother was, in her own words, sick as a dog. Like so many women before and after her, she adjusted. Every morning she threw up then walked slowly to the bus stop. She worked queasily through her day, felt better by evening, went to bed after dinner, slept the sleep of the dead, woke in the morning, and promptly threw up.

Historically, morning sickness has been attributed to both physiological and psychological factors. Rising hormone levels, especially estrogen and human chorionic gonadotropin (hCG), are thought to contribute to nausea and vomiting, but no one knows exactly how or why these cause gastrointestinal disturbance. Nor is it clear why morning sickness is more prevalent in younger rather than older mothers, nor why those women who experience some degree of morning sickness seem to bear a lower rate of miscarriage and a higher ratio of babies free of birth defects. One Swedish study postulated that the metamorphosis of the maternal digestive system, designed to help the body retain fat and process energy and nutrients more efficiently, may cause the release of hormones that contribute to the symptoms of morning sickness.

In fact, there may be an evolutionary advantage to morning sickness. In the days before pasteurization, refrigeration, and sanitation, food-borne parasites posed a severe threat to the health of the newly pregnant mother and embryo. For the same reasons pregnant women are advised to avoid unpasteurized cheeses, rare meat, and raw fish, prudent women in premodern times avoided bacteria-carrying foods, especially in the early, most vulnerable stages of gestation. (My dentist advised me not to have my teeth cleaned during the first trimester, lest harmful bacteria be absorbed into my blood stream.) Women who were too sick to eat or were revolted by especially dangerous food would have had a greater chance of carrying a healthy baby to term.

The psychological origins of morning sickness have been hypothesized largely as the result of placebo studies. Studies have attributed morning sickness to everything from ambivalence regarding the pregnancy to over-identification with the maternal role (or with one's own mother) to unconscious repudiation of the pregnancy, or of the baby's father, or of sex. This is not to suggest that morning sick women are out of their minds. Quite the contrary. One study linked a higher incidence of morning sickness with lessened incidence of psychological problems throughout pregnancy—as if morning sickness were not simply a psychosomatic phenomenon but a psychological and somatic solution to its radical transformation, a way to confront directly the emotional upheaval of pregnancy. In fact, while no woman who experiences these symptoms would brook the suggestion that the illness is all in her mind, if a sane woman truly understood the changes overtaking her body and soul, were she capable of knowing, consciously, exactly, just how the lines of her universe were being redrawn, no doubt the effect would be the same: she would grow faint, and heave and retch and purge, over and over again, simultaneously revolting from and making room for the alien within.

My sickness rendered me quite lifeless, except for the life deep inside me. Despite my misery, this grain of life inspired a kind of joy and deep content. I knew there would be a payoff, a pearl of a thing grown by this foreign irritant. That was the rub: while I told everyone that yes, I was sick, I didn't process my condition as illness. Rather, I felt my body at work. Years of dance training behind me made me keenly aware that this was the hardest work my body had ever done. From the age of eight I had taken myself first weekly, then biweekly, then daily to a dance studio, where I learned to control and flex and lift and turn every part of my body. I stretched my leg against the bar so I could maintain easily three perfect splits, lay in a splayed frog position to push the turn-out in my hips, endured long adagio combinations that made my legs shake underneath me, and repeated allegros until I could no longer achieve a single jump. Later came long days of rehearsals, my aching muscles warmed into life under plastic pants and leg warmers. I cross-trained with weights in order to strengthen my core and bolster my endurance. And in my recent training with Kory, I had pushed new limits, learning how to dance for hours in wedged heels and mastering intricate slides and aerial lifts in which I was quite literally thrown across the floor or over and around my husband's head. I loved to dance; I loved how dance had made me intimate with my body, its possibilities and limitations; I loved the hard work and the way my body responded to training; I loved even the pain that came when I pushed too hard. I loved especially the freedom of movement the work rewarded. So I thought I knew every muscle in my body. I thought I knew what it meant to do hard physical work. But what I thought was very, very wrong.

When you are pregnant no internal system, no muscle, no ligament, no joint or organ is spared. Every moment of me was pregnant, working deliberately as a Swiss watch. I could wallow in the nausea or I could try to fight it, but for all intents and purposes I had nothing to do with the pregnancy and I could do nothing about it.

This was lucky, because the sickness of early pregnancy made me irretrievably stupid. It was hard to think. With my brain as well as my gut shrouded in a hormonal fog, words eluded me. I forgot, literally, what day of the week it was. My body craved sleep. As often as I could, I lay in the afternoon sun and gazed blankly out the window. Occasionally I would try to read, slowly, lazily, but soon the words ran off the page. Generating another being was all my body—and imagination—could handle. Most of the time I felt there was no "I"—only a body that had taken over the space where my personality had once been.

This was, at first, one of the more astonishing and interesting aspects of pregnancy: it involved no thought. The baby barrels away, growing blithely in spite of you. Research could give me a mental picture but it could not describe how I felt; it could not approximate the oddness, the surreal experience of it. There was only this unfamiliar thing: a tiny bean in my belly, quite at home as far as it was concerned but quite a new and unfamiliar lodger to my body, which had been completely disrupted by its presence. In fact, although the fertilized egg is tiny, no thicker than a piece of typing paper, it is relatively massive, the largest cell in the human body. As I got sicker and sicker I took my state as a sign that things were working as they should, that my body knew what to do.

As I learned about what was happening in those early weeks, the common complaints—morning sickness, fatigue, even misery—they all made sense. The very tangible symptoms that had taken over my life were merely a sideshow. The real circus was within.

The development of the embryo proceeds rapidly. Within hours the single cell formed by the fusion of the egg and sperm has divided; after a week the embryo has blasted its way into the lining of the uterus, creating a small wound from which it finds its first external source of nourishment.

For the first weeks of its life the embryo is nothing more than a tube, comprised of three distinct layers of cells that will differentiate into brain, skin, nerves, muscles, blood, bones, stomach, lungs, and heart. Then, sometime around the fourth week, the ends of the tube begin to fold, curving in on themselves like fiddle ferns. One fold becomes the head, the other the baby's bottom. Two weeks later four bumps emerge, like tiny paddles: the beginnings of arms and legs. The head, with its indented eyespots, looks something like a head. As seen in pictures, six-week-old fetuses will bow their heads humbly over their middles. Hand paddles, with fingers already projecting, cradle their bulging hearts. In photographs they appear pale pink or amber, translucent with a tracing of feathery red veins. They are masses of prehistory a quarter of an inch long, with snouts and fluted stumps, but already the body bears the shadow of a human creature.

Yet these plastic manipulations of form and mutations of shape are not the only nor even the most remarkable development of early pregnancy. By week six the neural tube, which will become the spinal cord, has already developed. The nerve for the brain, visible through the fetal skin only seven weeks after conception, has formed. Lungs, kidneys, intestines, reproductive organs—all have begun to appear. The heart, originally begun as two parts, fuses and begins to beat. By the end of the second month of pregnancy the two-inch-long embryo, having developed all of the organs it will need for life—the entirety of its basic structural plan—has become a fetus.

It was something about the brain and the heart that got to me. The fact that these most vital of organs, organs I thought of as central (at least metaphorically) to mind and to soul, were already formed and working in those early weeks: this fact seemed to me impossible. So it made perfect sense that the baby made me sick. To create a brain was no small feat. To have grown a heart, a working heart so small that it could lodge like a splinter in an inch-long embryo, surely this was a task far larger than could be contained by my very average body. I stopped wondering why pregnant women got sick. Instead, I wondered how any of us didn't.

It was around this time, ten weeks or so, that we had our first doctor's appointment. Stacks of parenting magazines lay on the table, and Kory thumbed through one while I filled out the intake forms and questionnaires. Most of the required information was predictable: name, address, date of birth, medical history. Some was not: Do you have a partner/spouse? Do you feel adequately supported in this pregnancy? Are you happy about this pregnancy? What have you eaten in the past twenty-four hours?

At the reception desk we were handed a packet in a simple white folder, pockets neatly filled with printed matter, containing information that suddenly I craved: "Starting Out: Common Discomforts of Pregnancy"; "Danger Signs"; "Baby's Month-to-Month Development"; "Pregnancy and Breastfeeding Diet Guide"; "Anemia"; "Kegel Exercises"; "Prenatal Exercise and Back Care Handbook"; "What Every Woman Should Know about Breastfeeding"; "Reading List for Expectant Parents." I pulled one sheet after another out of the folder and read hungrily, in turn passing each sheet to Kory, who sat beside me and read with the same mad focus.

Eat small frequent meals. . . . Consume dry starch (crackers, toast, cereal) in the morning before you get out of bed. . . . A sudden change of position can aggravate nausea. . . . Notify your provider at once if you develop persistent vomiting, chills or fever, blurred vision, sudden swelling of hands or face. . . . If you bleed anytime during your pregnancy, have someone telephone your provider. . . . A woman's breasts increase in size during pregnancy, enlarging even more with sexual arousal. For some women this is the first time that they truly enjoy having their breasts fondled. . . . By the end of eight weeks . . . all the major internal organs have developed . . . facial features become more defined and brain development is well under way. By this time the embryo has grown to nearly two inches.

Finally we were ushered into a small exam room where we were met by an intern: a young, blonde, foreign-born but U.S.-trained medical student. She was thin with a fresh round face and a lovely musical accent. She was contemplating an OB/GYN specialty. Her smile was warm but she chattered nervously as she greeted us. She congratulated us once, then again. I sat waiting on the exam table. My husband rested quietly in the single chair next to the doctor's desk. I had the distinct impression that I was this girl's first pregnant patient. Not a one of us—not me, not she, certainly not Kory—knew exactly what we were supposed to do. She questioned me as if I actually knew something about my condition. "Are you feeling okay?" she wanted to know. And, "Have you experienced anything unusual?" And,

"Do you need anything specific from us today?" Although I was ignorant of procedure—and pretty much everything else—as I watched this young, bright-eyed, seemingly virginal girl, I felt the weight of my now-gravid body and it felt something like knowledge.

When she finally began the examination, her touch was light and fluttering. "Do your breasts always feel like this?" she asked.

"Yes," I lied, not sure what "like this" meant.

Our doctor, when she arrived, proved to be the doctor this young woman must have aspired to become. A sturdy, confident woman, she carried the unspoken assurance that she had delivered countless babies and had ushered thousands of mothers gracefully into and out of their pregnancies. "Let's do the fun part," she said, pulling out the transducer, a small handheld stethoscope that could amplify the loud, slow pulse of my own heart and the faster, higher tone of my baby's. She lowered it to my abdomen and I held my breath, unconsciously, as I would at every appointment to follow, and we listened. The heartbeat was not yet audible, and before I knew there was such a thing she had wheeled in a portable ultrasound and dimmed the lights. There, on the small screen, was our baby. A little bean of light with a heartbeat, a tiny pulse throbbing away, the faintest trail of the umbilical cord floating up through the darkness of my womb like a glowing skein. The room hushed and brimmed with the respectful silence that might fill a church or attend the arrival of royalty. As we four watched, becalmed, the very room seemed to me enchanted.

Our doctor talked our intern through the pelvic exam, expertly showed her my uterus, how it was beginning to bulge like a soft small pillow. She anticipated all of our questions: exercise, sex, a lengthy discussion of prenatal testing options. And then it was over.

The pregnancy was official. Also, unremarkable. Every bewildering thing that had thrust us into this uncharted place was part of an old familiar story. What had seemed unique, unparalleled, even miraculous to my newly forming mother's mind was, in fact, replicated daily in women all over the world. I was just another pregnant woman. Which was probably the most remarkable thing of all.

TESTED

At thirty-five I was a member of a definitive, well-studied medical category: a woman of advanced maternal age. These days it is impossible not to know that age is not a friend to pregnant women, and the early days of my pregnancy happened to coincide with a veritable media blitz on the subject. Daily papers, weekly newsmagazines, evening television journals—all were full of information regarding the risks of bearing children by women like me. But it was also easy to only half-hear the warnings, what with all those celebrities and all those older mothers who gathered in local parks with their multiples. Every woman I met in my prenatal yoga class, in every birth class I would take, all of them, were in their thirties. Many were approaching or had passed thirty-five. We knew we were at risk so we made it our business to acquaint ourselves with the variety of tests at our disposal: nuchal translucency, amniocentesis, chorionic villus sampling, the mandatory (and highly unreliable) alpha-fetoprotein screening. We spoke glibly of our experiences and their results, using acronyms and cryptic numbers, giving meaningful nods to ratios and statistics. NT, CVS, AFP, triple screen, amnio. It was as if our fluency in this secret language meant something, as if mastering the code had some correlation with a successful, healthy pregnancy. We seemed to think that the knowledge of the medical business engulfing us had the power to wrest control of the situation back from our bodies. Almost every woman I knew during my early pregnancy took one or more of these tests; we talked among ourselves in that endless and covenish way of all first-time mothers because we had chosen to gamble, and we knew it. We had all hoped for a stockpile of biological time, a quantity very different from and fundamentally more urgent than real time. We all prayed, in both secular and sacred ways, that our babies were healthy and whole. But we knew the risks, and the divide between knowing the statistics and suddenly realizing that they did, in fact, apply to us was like confronting the disjunction between theory and practice. While you may think you know how to pray, that knowledge is imperfect until you have bowed down on your knees and given full voice to the hymn in your soul. So it was for me as I considered the health of my unborn baby. Abstract facts became urgent, pressing realities. In those first weeks I worried a lot.

In the United States one in eight hundred births will be a Down syndrome child, but the risk increases exponentially with the mother's age. Between the ages of thirty and forty the risk a woman faces for trisomy 21, the clinical name for Down syndrome, rises at an alarming rate: from less than .1 percent at age thirty, to .2 percent at thirty-four, .5 percent at thirty-eight, and .7 percent at thirty-nine, until a woman over forty has a greater than 1 percent chance of conceiving and carrying a Down syndrome baby. By age fifty the risk will have risen to 15 percent. Put another way, while a twenty-year-old had a less than 1 in 1500 chance of having a Down syndrome baby, my chance was greater than 1 in 300, with a total risk for "clinically significant chromosome abnormalities" of about 1 in 150. I knew, of course, that these numbers also meant that there was more chance than not that my baby would be healthy. But I still didn't like the numbers and I didn't like the rising curve of risk.

There are other, rarer chromosomal deformities, too, like trisomy 13 and trisomy 18. These are considered "viable" abnormalities because the fetus may be carried to term. But such children pay a high price. Most often they will have serious congenital heart defects and eating disorders. They may have severe mental retardation. The mortality rate for trisomy 18 babies is 90 percent by age one. Other chromosomal deformities are so debilitating that no one knows what they look like because the fetus cannot be carried to term.

Most days I did not think I could bear to give up my life for a lifetime of care. Other days I knew that I would jettison everything, throw over my life, and live like Jonah in the belly of the whale if asked to tend to my sick or disabled child. I worried intensely, fearing that old proverb: God does not give you anything you cannot bear. Kory was sober but confident. He professed simply that he would love whatever came our way. Not being a person of spiritual faith, he nevertheless had a deep reserve of compassion, even forbearance. For this I was deeply grateful but not terribly relieved.

In the twelfth week of the pregnancy we went for a nuchal translucency test. At the time a relatively new test in the United States, nuchal translucency is a highly precise ultrasound that screens for Down syndrome, major heart and neural tube disorders, and two other chromosomal defects. Using technology developed in Great Britain, the technician takes precise measurements of the fetus, including a measurement of the amount of fluid in the base of the fetus's neck. By considering that measurement alongside the mother's age and the age of the fetus, the test can pinpoint with great accuracy the risk the fetus has of developing these particular defects. While the technique is advanced and highly precise, the science behind it is surprisingly simple. Down syndrome babies tend to have decreased circulatory systems, and it seems that because of the position of the fetus *in utero*, fluid generally accumulates in large quantities at the base of the fetus's neck. The more fluid measured, the higher the risk of defect. While the NT cannot diagnose any single condition and thus cannot tell you the health of your baby with complete accuracy, it can give you a very good estimation of the likelihood your child will have one of these conditions. More important to us, the noninvasive NT test can reassure or alert you to problems much earlier than can an amniocentesis—a test normally not done before the sixteenth week. By the sixteenth week the second trimester of the pregnancy is well underway, and should the mother decide to terminate, she faces the rather difficult proposition of a second trimester abortion. Already I knew what was inside me, and it was a knowledge not culled from books or dialogue but from something deep and irrefutable. After a lifetime of pro-choice sentiment and left-wing activism on many political fronts, I could no longer think abstractly about abortion as an impersonal, democratic, or even feminist right. It was still all those things for me, and I still categorically believed that all women ought to have choice and reproductive freedom as well, away from state (and church) interference with their bodies. But now that I was pregnant it was also equally categorically true that I believed I had a baby inside of me and I could not bear to think about ending its life. For the first time in my life I thought about it that simply. Pregnancy made me think reductively, at least in my own case, even though I recognized that what was true for me was not necessarily true for other women in vastly different circumstances. These two true things—I had a baby, I had a right to choose—made all the statistics and all the risks real. And urgent.

On the morning of the nuchal translucency we ascended to the genetics department of our university hospital, which occupied the uppermost floor of one of the tallest buildings on campus. As we sat in that ethereal waiting room high above the city, I was instructed to drink three glasses of water to help push my uterus forward and clarify the sonogram. We sat and spoke neither to each other nor to the other couples who wandered quietly in. This was not a room for joyful pregnant banter nor for congratulatory hails. We were all there for the same, primitive reason: we were scared.

In my nerviness, the occasion seemed momentous. Even the name of the test, as it turned over and over in my mind, seemed foreign and marvelous, as new and technologically improbable as a journey to Mars. My anxiety was raw and palpable, not unlike the fear of flying that had recently possessed me. As I sat, cradled snugly in the armchair, it was like sitting alone in the seat of a plane, waiting for the slow taxi, the gravid gathering of speed, and the sudden, horrible loss of ground below. Fear ricocheted inside me: who knew what to expect once the ground fell away? In that weightful moment, who could possibly predict what life or what death awaited you?

Kory and I sat side by side, not touching, not talking, not doing much of anything but waiting in that horrible silence. I drank my water and stared out the window. Kory paged silently through entertainment tabloids. He seemed oblivious to everything around him. We tried not to think because everything seemed a likely trap. If we broached the subject of pregnancy, the specter of disease and disability was right there, through those doors. If we broached another topic, well, how could you even think of such a thing at a time like this? We waited for what seemed hours until finally it was our turn, then we marched dutifully through that door, my body feeling the full weight of the pregnancy.

The genetics counselor took a family history and, using little wormy diagrams of chromosomes, showed us pictorially what defects and abnormalities looked like on the chromosomal level. The marks wiggled across the page in neat rows, inchworm twins, mealworm triplets, each signifying a human gene gone terribly wrong. Though the lines spelled no clear or exact picture of *baby*, I read each one distinctly: failed possibility; My brain won't grow; My spine is hollow; I can't walk; Help, I can't talk; Help me breathe; My heart is broken. . . . With so many mutations, so many vulnerable, fragile threads of genetic matter, it hardly seemed possible that a round mass of cells, tinier than a mote in my eye, could conspire to become something like me or my husband or the woman who explained it all to us.

As she turned page after page, there was so much to consider. So many complicated maps and patterns, so many places for chromosomal tails to break off, for two to become three, for long buried traits to reappear. Had I married adequate genetic material? What did I know about my husband, really? Or myself, for that matter? How did anyone emerge from that darkness whole? How did one, single healthy sperm out of millions *ever* manage to swim its way all the way to the well-formed egg? My mind boiled, a whitewater of possibilities, and then it shut down. A cascade of fear and darkness or a cataract of joy was rushing toward us and nothing could change the outcome.

We were ushered into a warm, dim room. I lay semi-reclined on the table. I lifted my shirt, lowered the waist of my pants. Warm, viscous conducting fluid squirted onto my abdomen. The technician armed herself with the transducer and, with a few deft strokes, found the baby.

It had grown. The little heart flickered away like a Christmas light; it was strong and sure as a beacon. No longer a bean, the baby now had a head, and legs, and arms, and it danced in its watery sac. The technician scanned and the baby moved, unwilling to keep still, kicking and punching and twisting. It was restless, turning side to side. For a moment it played possum, and a shadowy gray-white being hovered in the center of the dark screen. We drank in the image.

Sitting beside me in the dark, his chair pulled close to my head, Kory started. "Oh," he said with such genuine, subdued surprise that it confirmed the astonishment welling within me.

"It's very cute," said the technician.

Kory leaned over me, intently watching the screen. I cradled his head against my chest. We were as intimate as we had ever been, joined to each other and to the light-filled form that danced before us. We were both humbled, returned to something primitive and sacred. All that technology surrounded us but we saw only the simple, irreducible fact of our child, of two becoming one, of something from (nearly) nothing, the sentiment and cliché of it, the predictability of it, the startling newness of it. Already something had begun to change in us, between us.

On the screen the technician captured a quick succession of images: a profile, a hand, a close-up of the head.

And then, kick! A quick, agile flip from right to left. There had never been movement so surprising, so miraculous. Tiny feet punched the air, arms reached up, out, testing the dark, liquid world. I thought: *It can move.* I thought: *I might feel it.* "Can you feel that?" Kory wondered. And it seemed impossible to both of us that I couldn't. "Really?" he asked. But although I held my breath and focused all of my attention on the thing that I could see so clearly right there on the screen in front of us, I felt nothing. Inside me there was only stillness, and while this quiet was now charged with possibility and the bright shadow of that almost-human form, that bud of light remained another uncanny fact of those early weeks, another disjunction between what I knew and what I felt, between what was happening inside me and what I looked like on the outside.

After, the results were immediate. The risks were sufficiently low to warrant no further tests, and the anxieties of the past weeks, both overt and subconscious, were washed away with the last stickiness of the conducting fluid. Outside I felt brighter, as if life as well as light had dilated my eyes. Now I could return to the business of being normally, unremarkably pregnant.

"Now will you stop worrying?" Kory asked quietly as we walked to the car. His arm was around me, and he was smiling.

"Yes," I exhaled. "Now I know for sure."

"Good," he said. "I wasn't worried, but this is better."

Propelled by relief, I nearly danced down the street.

Many weeks later, at the second ultrasound, we lingered over the baby for a long time.

It was a more clinical portrait than the first, and we watched as the technician scanned and measured organs, mapped the baby's size onto my due date: the brain, two grape-sized nodes, seen from above; the long spindly spine; the arch of the rib cage and its thin but precisely formed bones; the hole of the stomach, filled with amniotic fluid; the kidneys, seen in cross section; the kernel of the heart, pumping tirelessly away (seen from every imaginable angle); the arms and legs, ever squirming. The profile was sharp and clear: a button nose, two closed eyes, the mouth, a minute, flickering tongue.

Kory had a much easier time making out the parts. An artist, he is trained to look and, in looking, to understand. He made sense of it, of those Rorschach blots of organs. He held my hand again, he helped me to see. We marveled that all the parts were there, including the clear and shapely V where her legs met, her lovely little girl parts.

No Baryshnikov, no Balanchine could have startled grace into me like those first pictures of my baby. Each time I had expected a doll, a still picture, not something with a life of its own. But there she was, lively and strong. So independent, so much an entity unto herself. She moved. It was that simple. That simple fact made her real.

As I watched my baby bounce inside of me I had thought for a brief moment that I shouldn't dance. Then I thought I should dance as much as I could so that the baby would grow to love movement and music as much as we did. I imagined that already she had a personality. That perhaps, during the first ultrasound, she had been mad or restless, uncomfortable or curious. That she was stretching her newly sprouted limbs, learning what it meant to have a body. I wondered if she was what woke me in the early morning hours, sending me unconscious signals, letting me know she was already a night owl like her father.

Then I understood why, for centuries, women had felt that pregnancy was an alien thing. Pregnancy is a deeply visceral experience, completely and utterly physical. But it is also transcendent, mystical. That was the odd disjunction of viewing those first pictures: there was a baby, moving, material, incontrovertibly real. She was a fact. Nevertheless, it was difficult to believe in this fact. All I really knew was how much I loved her. The rest of it seemed impossible, unreal. Yet in that first hour, as I watched the vision of the sonogram, the baby became fully our child—*A person! A pronoun! You!* As I gazed and gazed, I regained my infant sight.

PUBLIC LIFE

Almost imperceptibly, as I approached the end of the first trimester my energy returned, and with it came a new kind of elation. Hormones played on my system like friendly demons. At night I was restless and wakeful, unable to penetrate the deepest barriers of sleep. I became an insomniac, able to sleep only three or four hours at a time. I was soon intimately acquainted with the still hours between three and six a.m., when even the caged pit bull next door, that often growled and barked all day, was silent. In those hours, the only moving thing was my mind, and it was turned inward, a vortex of frettings and fantasies. I thought about practical things: cribs, christenings, changing tables, linens, clothes, toys, monitors. I wondered about motherhood, the reckless responsibility of it. I wondered what my daughter would look like, what she would become, and what would become of me. I thought about nothing, too, emptying my mind of every conscious moment that indicated me to myself. I let the Blank envelope me, as if I myself were in a womb. Although my husband lay beside me, it was a supremely solitary time, as if my daughter and I were the only ones in the universe. Then, in the very early morning, just before my husband woke for work, or sometimes much later, in the afternoon, warm and wrapped in blankets on the living room couch, I often fell into a deep and pleasurable sleep that brought dreams and restfulness. I woke from these naps slowly, as if returning from another world, as if I had actually visited that place where the baby lived, as if I had once again met myself and remembered who, exactly, I was.

By the thirteenth week a small, hard bump swelled from my stomach. An impertinent lump, it didn't yield when I pressed on it but remained firm and compact. I thought, irrationally: *It is beginning.*

Around this time, too, my appetite returned. I knew I was recovering on the November night I felt well enough to cook. Outside, it was cold and dark, already winter. I rummaged through my pantry like a squirrel checking her winter's store, assessing what I had purchased from the farmers market in hopes that, this week, I might be able to eat. For the first time in months the ingredients in my cupboard suggested tastes that I craved, smells that I welcomed. In the kitchen I chopped, stirred, and sautéed. The pleasures of my knives and my favorite pan seemed like small epiphanies. I cooked sweet onions and buttery red chard, tangy cranberries mellowed with brown sugar and red wine, tender pork loin and heirloom dumpling squash. As I sat at the table with my husband and ate a proper dinner properly, I suddenly realized that I was famished. It was the first meal I had enjoyed in months, and every bite seemed a return to life.

Pregnant women are often very, very hungry, and not simply for food. Their desires can seem unreasonable and patently irrational to the non-pregnant, spouses included. There is a kind of mania that can overtake a pregnant woman, and once the fatigue of the first trimester subsides, it is not unusual for her to become obsessed, as I did in those dark hours, with her home, with organizing her life, with preparing for the advent of the new child. It's called the nesting instinct, and while it's often strongest in the final months, it can be present in the earliest months as well. Like so many other things about pregnancy, no one is really sure what causes nesting, but most suspect it is induced in part by hormones, in part by psyche. The nesting urge is not limited to humans: birds, hamsters, bears—all manner of mammals prepare in some way for the coming of their broods. In other words, pregnant humans are not crazy. This primal, evolutionary urge might compel them to wash, organize, disinfect, scrub, donate, expel, redesign. It's another one of those altered states that pregnant women are so good at entering and which makes sense only to them.

As a writer and academic I was trained, for better and for worse, to think about things endlessly, comprehensively, and from every angle, to research those things I didn't understand fully. It made perfect sense that much of my obsession with pregnancy and becoming a mother was psychological. I simply could not stop thinking about what was happening to me, what would come next, how I might (better) prepare for the baby. I read voraciously. Other, less anxious women forgo these mental gyrations and exhibit strong, even compulsive practical behaviors. A pregnant woman can look around a perfectly beautiful home and see only disorder, dust, and waste. She might feel ashamed to bring a child into the chaos she suddenly perceives around her—even though the same life felt perfectly satisfactory just a month before. So she tidies and cleans until her home sparkles. She might redecorate, reorganize drawers and closets, hang wallpaper, or paint. A woman at church confided to me, "In my ninth month, I was on my hands and knees, scrubbing my kitchen floor."

As my pregnancy progressed I was possessed by an overwhelming impulse for control, as if organizing my space would somehow enable me to control the life which was about to be wrenched from me. There was not much in our apartment to organize (though I would reconsider this fact in later months when my mania reached a fever pitch) and not much we could do to redecorate our rented space. We had chosen our flat in part because it was simple. It consisted of two bedrooms, one used as an office, and one bathroom. It had white walls and a palatable neutral carpet; a reasonably functional galley kitchen with a gas range and sufficient cabinet space; and a large living-dining area framed by a modern-style bay window. The large backyard supported fantastic geranium bushes with ponderous crimson blooms and several raised boxes in which I grew vast amounts of arugula, the only produce that really thrived in the foggy, damp air. It was a flat typical of San Francisco's far western Sunset district, home mostly to surfers and immigrant Chinese families. It was not much of a community for us, but the flat was clean, affordable, and available (an unusual triumvirate at the time), and our landlady, Mabel, was a warm if eccentric Chinese woman who took good care of us when she wasn't moving furniture in the middle of the night. The building was two blocks from the beach, a luxury that became an indispensible part of our life's rhythm.

We had filled the apartment with Kory's art, my books, and a few new pieces of furniture: a Mission-style sofa and coffee tables, and a beautiful white hutch for our dishes and growing collection of glassware. It had begun to feel like home, but it was so simple that there was little to be done in the way of remodeling. When it was time for the baby, we would move our office into a corner of the living room and transform the extra room into the nursery. But the fourth month was still too early for that.

Instead of redecorating, I wrote lists. I wrote epic, detailed, satisfying lists that organized every aspect of our life. I listed work tasks, and home tasks, and errands; I listed what I ate, what I wanted to eat, the meals for the week, cookbooks to consult, ingredients for meals, which stalls at the market would have those ingredients; I listed the baby gear we'd need, prenatal tasks to be accomplished, how to organize our small home office; I listed bills to be paid, books to be read, coursework to prepare. What did I need? Want? Fantasize about? I found a way to make a list. And then, one day, I planned a party.

We were among the first in our immediate social circle to be married and the first by many years to have a baby. We had told the news to our families and a very few of our closest friends (all of whom lived out of town), but not wanting to offer explanation were I suddenly to find myself not pregnant, we followed common practice—a superstition, really, among first-time mothers—and we kept the pregnancy a secret. Yet, as the months wore on and the pregnancy became the major fact of my existence, it became difficult not to reveal it. In casual social situations I was constantly distracted. Nothing much mattered but my body and the baby, nor did I want to talk about much of anything else. I felt duplicitous, and soon the urge to tell became so overwhelming that I started to avoid my friends, the phone, my email account. Once the results of the NT were safely behind us, though, it seemed silly not to share our news. So, as the first trimester ended, we turned our sights outward and began preparations to go public. To this day I'm not quite sure what we were thinking, nor what possessed me to plan a large party on the heels of an exhausting semester of teaching and morning sickness. I'm not sure why we felt the need to announce the news rather than tell our friends one by one and let word spread naturally, as word will. I suspect, though, that as our social circle was so wide at the time and the news was so astonishing (even—or especially—to us), we felt compelled to celebrate. Somehow we thought the ceremony of it would make it real. Maybe then the pregnancy would become something we could own instead of something we simply wondered about.

In early November I began to review cookbooks and clippings, my own notes, journals, and memories for inspiration. I'd collected menus for years, from mom-and-pop joints to some of the finest restaurants in the country. Many of them were signed by the chef, framed and hung on the walls of our dining room. Now I studied these and combed through others, looking for dishes and presentation ideas. What made a meal coherent and memorable? I knew that it wasn't simply the food. The woodcuts that adorned my Chez Panisse menus embodied their reverence for the natural world, their sophisticated artisanal aesthetic. An early handwritten menu from Prune was signed in hot pink highlighter, with Gabrielle Hamilton's command, "Eat Meat!" It made sense alongside her bold, eclectic take on rustic Italian cooking. Arnolfo, in Tuscany, announced elegantly one more fantastic dish after another in foreign-looking script. The version I had been given, and which hung now in our home, had no prices. I resolved that our party would not be the potluck-bring-your-own-booze-eat-off-paper-with-plastic affair that large gatherings easily became among our friends. This party would be different.

I sat at our dining room table, surrounded by books and clippings and loose papers, and devoted a fresh notebook to the task. I brainstormed themes, referenced my favorite cookbooks, and drafted courses with the fervor I had once devoted to dissertation research. In my notebook I linked courses with serving pieces, scheduled the prep work, listed the cleaning and imagined the decorating. For a month I surveyed our small apartment, our collection of plates, flatware, and serving dishes. Several times a day I gauged what I could serve, where, and how. There would be at least thirty guests, and I was hell-bent on serving them dinner.

Because something possessed me to make a fresh pâté de campagne, which is at least a week-long process, I settled on a rustic

French menu with coq au vin as the centerpiece. To start we'd have two mousses: tuna and salmon, a celery salad with anchovy vinaigrette, the pâté and bread, and several bowls of good olives. The coq au vin would serve everyone from one large enameled cast iron pot, with a large side of steamed and buttered green beans. Knives would be unnecessary. For dessert we would have chocolate roulade, a deceptively simple but intensely chocolate affair, and I'd put my labor instead into candied oranges, which required several more days of steeping, sugaring, and drying. I'd have champagne and bourbon milk punch (which wasn't at all French but was a holiday tradition) and a few bottles of good red wine for everyone but me. I figured most would be too busy eating and drinking to notice that I wasn't.

I opened new files on the computer and designed menus and invitations, which we sent by mail. This put some of our friends on notice that something was going on, but since a having a baby was so completely foreign to our world, this possibility occurred only in passing, to only one friend. A full page of my notebook listed tasks by day for the final week leading up to the party.

Ten days before:
   Assemble pâté and marinate meats
Sunday:
   Make candied oranges
   Cut bread and freeze
   Marinate pâté meat
Monday:
   Cook pâté
   Set out candles
   Clean desk in office for bar space
   Polish ice bucket
   Label platters
   Gather baskets, napkins, etc.
   Sugar oranges

Tuesday:
    Make tuna mousse
    Make chocolate sauce
    Make bourbon milk punch
    Sugar oranges again

Yet, even with an entire week devoted to planning and prep cooking, Friday's list comprised an entire page of final details: wash floors, chill champagne, light candles. . . .

We bought holiday napkins, a beautiful ruby red ribbon garland for the tree, dozens of new punch glasses. We inventoried our Christmas decorations—the table runners and angel candles and miniature Santa statues, our family mangers. We finally got rid of the tackiest ornaments and put out a careful selection of only the most beautiful or those that had accumulated meaning for us. Kory made Christmas cookies for favors, little jeweled treats, and boxed them in miniature holly-printed takeout containers. Our invitation list grew. I despaired of seating everyone.

As the date approached, I cleaned for a week and cleared the clutter out of the bathroom, the office, the living room, the entry hall, even the tops of bookcases. We actually washed the crown molding, standing on chairs, then on our landlady's borrowed ladder, and we finally framed and hung our wedding photos. I put candles in the crystal candlesticks for the first time and set them on the dining table.

The Sunday after Thanksgiving, the weekend before the party, we bought our Christmas tree. We were the first customers at the lot, which had only just opened that morning, and I was only slightly ashamed of our puppy dog eagerness. The lot, surrounded by a high, chain-link fence on a busy city thoroughfare, was one of many opportunistic businesses that sprang up during holiday seasons to hawk trees, pumpkins, or flowers. The remaining months of the year the lot was filled with patches of brown, scrappy grass and potholed asphalt. The experience was exactly the opposite of driving over the bridge to the acres of tree farms that graced the coastal lands of Half Moon Bay, where Santa waited for the kids and bounce houses were staffed by elves to provide after-tree chopping distraction. There was to be none of that family-memory-making nostalgia for me. I wanted the tree and I wanted it now.

We paced row after row of trees while the cars whizzed by on 19th Avenue. All of them were healthy and beautiful, but I made Kory rotate a dozen for me so I could be sure that our tree would be perfect.

Finally, we tied the Noble Fir to the roof of our car and drove home slowly against a gusty but strangely warm November wind. The tree rocked precariously against the roof of the car, and I smelled the damp sea air through the open window. It was nothing like Christmas, but neither was I anything like myself. The wind was the kind that blew clouds with an almost super-natural force, and that afternoon the sky was vast and change-able. I was unsettled and ecstatic, though this had nothing to do with the weather.

Kory hauled the tree up our narrow entryway. It shed a thick rug of needles on the stairs and across our living room carpet. The pile of green needles grew over the next half hour as I de-bated where, exactly, to place the tree. "Try it in front of the bay window," I said.

"Here?" Kory asked.

"No! Off to the corner!" As Kory dragged the tree inch by inch to its next potential spot, he was stoic. He moved the fur-niture. He repositioned the tree. Soon, as needles showered his jacket, his silence took great effort of will. His mouth clamped into a thin line. Finally I approved the location, but then the tree had to be rotated on its vertical axis so I could discern the perfect tree viewing angle. Truly, I had no mind of my own but neither did he have the patience of a saint. "It's a fucking tree, Lisa!" he finally exclaimed, throwing up his hands. "It's going to be covered with things. NO ONE will see that one inch of bare spot." And he walked away. I took a deep breath. I grabbed the tree by its thick trunk and turned it a few more inches. I stepped back and put my hands on my hips. "That's fine," I said. Kory shook his head and got out the vacuum.

Five days later, white roses and evergreens filled our vases and fresh garlands graced the arched entryway to the living room and sloped across the tops of the bookshelves. The house smelled of cinnamon and pine and the table was filled with food and drink. Our guests arrived, and for the first time that week I had nothing to do. The coq au vin, which had taken two full days to prepare—browning and braising ten pounds of chicken myself, on my small stove—had been worth it, because now it simmered in the oven, its aroma filling our small flat with the promise of its earthy, wine-dark goodness. We talked, we ate, they drank. Since that night we've thrown many parties, with more elaborate menus and just as many people, but this night remains among the most perfect. Perhaps it was simply the spell cast by the hormones—or the maniacal planning the hormones had prompted—that had actually resulted in a perfect party. Or maybe it was because it was the first, or maybe it was because our friends at the time were a joyful, swing dancing bunch who knew how to have a good time. For all of these reasons I was relaxed and unburdened and able to enjoy the food, my friends, that very moment of being, surrounded by everything I loved. So I waited and my secret nested inside me, a silent guest.

Just before dinner we called our friends into the living room. We stood in front of the tree, and Kory put his arm around me. There was silence, then he told them. There was more stunned silence, then a cheer went round the room. We grinned. We kissed like we had just gotten engaged. Our friends cheered again. Our secret loosed, I felt myself expand and return to myself. Someone took a picture of us in front of the tree. I was three months pregnant and wore a skinny black velvet tank top and a pair of wide-legged black pants that pulled just a little against my middle, but I didn't exactly look pregnant. Kory stood beside me in a v-neck sweater and jeans, looking altogether the proud and happy cliché.

As we made our way toward dinner, our friends surrounded us. Certainly, I had expected good cheer. But their exuberance surprised me. Even our male friends were moved. "It takes a real man to have a baby," Johnny said. Paolo nodded and grinned. "Congratulations," he said. Tanoa grinned and nodded. "Wow, we're going to have a baby around. A little jitterbaby. That's going to be so fun." Others we would tell later had similar reactions. Pops, the singer of Swing Session and ever theatrical, threw his arms in the air and exclaimed, "Thank God!" Bowen, the band's drummer, smiled like the Cheshire cat; Little David just nodded. "Hey, that's cool," he said. Bowen and David were fathers themselves, so they knew something of what was in store for us. We weren't prepared for the enthusiasm, but we learned quickly that, like most people I would encounter during my pregnancy, our friends had insatiable goodwill regarding babies, and many had a surprising curiosity about pregnancy and childbirth. In fact, that night our friends seemed almost as interested in the details as we were. It was as if we had journeyed to a strange land and returned to tell about it. The baby rallied our friends. Was I sick? Had I gained weight? "I *thought* you had gained weight!" Kyle said, not so flatteringly. "I was looking at you in that shirt and I thought . . ." They wanted to know if we would move, if we knew the sex? Had we been trying? How long did we try? What were my symptoms? Could I feel it move yet? Were we excited?

One girlfriend—a pale, thin, rather arch young woman with

an exacting sense of style, who had professed her lack of interest in children to me months earlier—wanted to know the most. Even the most technical aspects of the pregnancy interested her: How big was it now? When would I feel it move? What did it look like on the ultrasound? (For this I retrieved those grainy chiaroscuro pictures.) How had I known? Did my boobs feel different? Another wanted to know how it felt to be pregnant, which fact I couldn't really describe except to say that (now that the morning sickness was over) it felt obscurely different and absolutely the same. I was myself, only more blissful. Everyone agreed that it would be fun to have a baby around. Later, because none of us could be in a room together for long without dancing, we pulled back the furniture and took our turns dancing in a small, cleared-away space in the middle of the living room. Even the friction of the carpet and constraint of the small space didn't dampen the energy, and when it was my turn to dance with Kory, we did a little hop-stepping basic, a few saucy kicks, and a freespin, then dragged it off to watch the others kick it up in their crazy, drunken way. We were grinning because, for the first time, it didn't matter so much how well we danced, just that we could do it together. "That was fun," Kory said to me, and I nodded.

The party was splendid. Our friends ate all of the food, stayed too late, and many of the men drank far more than they should have. I rescued a vintage hobnail ice cream dish from being used as a champagne flute, but they all sang in the street on the way to their cars.

The evening, that party, marked a turning point. Certainly, my body was different than it had been, but that night we were different, too. At the cusp of the second trimester, the party marked our entry into the world of the publicly, if not yet visibly, pregnant. Our private knowledge unfurled and rushed away from us like a receding wave or a sudden gust of wind. It transformed our landscape. We had announced the pregnancy to our friends but they had inadvertently announced something to us, too. Parenthood would create a new role for us, and our friends understood this better than we did. We were still ourselves, of course, but we were ourselves with something addended, something whose measure would be decisive if not yet tallied. If it was in my nature to want to know these things, it was in the nature of babies to remain unknown. So the insomnia, the Blank, the endless, exhausting planning and cleaning, these obsessive preparations were inevitable as I surveyed my deeply inadequate nest. I wanted to settle in. It was impossible to settle in. How could I settle when there was a stranger lurking just outside my door?

After the party I understood implicitly that motherhood would not be a private, domestic affair. It would also be public and joyful. Like all good parties, it would be spontaneous and unscripted, with all the pleasures that attend spontaneous and unscripted things (disappointments and disasters, too, quite possibly). As much as I might muse and fret and plan, motherhood's unfolding would be impossible to know, and it was cowardly for me to attempt to contain it. I might prepare but I could never plan. We would simply have to open our minds and hearts to our daughter as easily as we had opened our home to our old friends. We would put out a wide welcome then step over the threshold and invite her in.

PAS DE DEUX

Not many weeks later, fifteen weeks pregnant, I felt it. A quick one-two, a light fluttering punch. A surprise. A tease. A flirty call for attention: Hey, Mom! Look at me!

"Something moved," I said. We had been lounging impassively on the couch, but now Kory sat up quickly and placed his hand on my stomach. I tried not to breathe.

"Are you sure?" he asked, disbelieving. I was sure. I had been still, and in spite of me, inside me, something had moved, jolted, jumped. On the outside there was absolutely nothing to prove my claim, but I knew that something—*someone*—had moved. Rationally I knew she had moved before. We had both seen her on those ultrasounds. But something infinitely more primal and more immediate had happened on the couch, and its aftermath was not unlike the seconds after a small earthquake, when everything you know about the world is cast into doubt, when your own terra firma crumbles beneath you, and you are certain only of uncertainty.

In pregnancy your body moves without your knowing it. Your hamstrings tighten and contract. Your calves seize with odd and unaccountable cramps. In the tenth, fourteenth, thirty-second week, my body felt battered and worn, more taxed by the hormone relaxin than it had ever been by any dance class. Some mornings I woke to find my stomach sore, as if I had done a hundred crunches. It became hard to twist my torso, not because of my girth but because of the pain. My ankles, my knees, my shoulders, but most especially my hips, throbbed. All I wanted was to stretch, to rotate my hips and shoulders deep in their sockets. In the dark predawn I slid out of bed and squatted in the dark. I let my knees, my hips, my pelvic floor give way to gravity and the inevitable, literal widening and loosening of my joints. Years of dance training had taught me much about my body and movement and how a body learns to move. But it prepared me not at all for the absolute and startling newness of quickening, that moment when the pregnant woman first feels the baby move inside her. The term comes from the Old English *cwic*: living, live, alive. In modern terms it is an archaic notion, since modern technology can perceive life as well as movement long before the woman experiences it. But still, there is something extraordinary about the sensation of something living and moving inside of you, and there is something metaphorically startling in the conjoinment of those ideas: movement, life.

My dancing, my real life in dance, began the summer I was seven. I lay one afternoon on my parents' bed, dangling my feet over the edge. My mother was hanging a dress in her closet, my father changing his clothes. Blue paisley wallpaper danced up the walls, and I was possessed by the childhood calm of merely waiting and being. In this quiet unassuming moment, with her back turned to me, my mother asked a simple question: "Would you like to go to Garden State next year?"

Perhaps we had been talking about dancing, or perhaps I had been humming and kicking my feet with that incessant motion that courses through young bodies. The question, like so many others that issued from the faraway world of adults, was as unexpected as a snow day and even more welcome.

Garden State School of Ballet was a serious ballet school. Run by Fred Danielli, a former New York City Ballet dancer under George Balanchine, Garden State's main studio was some miles west, in the once vibrant but now embattled city of Newark. By some stroke of serendipity that I understood even as a child, there was a satellite school in my town. Even as a child I knew that professional dancers began their careers there.

I had never been inside the studio, which lay behind a glass door next to the town's renowned delicatessen. Sometimes, shopping downtown with my mother, I saw older girls, their hair coiled into important buns, their pale cardigans revealing a window of simple black leotard, legs long and pink in back-seamed tights. Bags stuffed with slippers, extra stockings, hairpins, even toe shoes, they slipped silently through the glass door. It was an ordinary enough door, but to me it might as well have been the entrance to Ali Baba's cave. I knew what transformations occurred within. At the top of those narrow stairs was a studio, a world where girls were taught to do complicated things with their feet. I longed to join them, but it seemed impossible that I would ever be old enough to attend.

In the silence that followed my mother's query I wondered: *How did they know?* I thought: *How could they not know?* I thought the world had been dropped at my feet.

"Yes," I said quietly. "I would love to go."

That fall, I entered the studio. I clutched the hem of my circle skirt, my stomach aflutter. Then I stood in the bright, narrow studio, opposite a bank of mirrors, leaning shyly as the other girls leaned shyly, against the triple rail of bars. The first thing we learned was never to lean against the bar. The second thing was never to wear skirts. We were sent out to our mothers, skirts hanging from our arms like wilted flowers.

Then, the positions. Feet. Arms. Feet and arms together. *Port de bras.* The deep bend of the knees: *plié*, to fold. The extension and point of the foot: *tendu*, to stretch. There were always two things: the dance and the language of the dance. We learned French, but the words themselves were not nearly so foreign as what they signified for our bodies. A small kick of the foot was paltry and weak compared to the staccato burst of a *dégagé*, disengaged, to strike. If we understood *grand plié*, the great fold, our bodies could sink magisterially, until we hovered just above the floor. It was as far from a squat as a puddle from the sea.

Because one cannot dance without knowing what motion to gather within, our minds were disciplined as well as our bodies. We remembered positions: first, second, third, fourth, fifth, *croisé, effacé, en face, écarté*, and movements: *coupé, jeté, rond de jambe, fondu, développé, pas de chat, grand jeté, tour jeté.* The words, exchanged among us like secret code, bestowed knowledge and real, physical power. We learned our first center combination and stood untethered from the bar, half terrified, half ecstatic at that liberty. We took our first movements across the floor, flooding the space with a rush of legs. We suffered our first pointe class, a slow, awkward initiation. There was no end to the vocabulary, nor to what we could ask our bodies to do.

One year, a new teacher stood before our class. I was ten, in a forest green leotard and pale pink tights. We stood facing the bar in first position and began class with a slow, simple *plié* sequence, then a series of deep *cambrés*. Suddenly, Christian stood behind me, his hands cupped around my rib cage. He urged my torso up, settled it gently into a higher place. Unconsciously my body responded. It lifted, opened, and found grace in a movement as thoughtless and essential as breath.

Christian was not a kind man. His classes were brutally difficult. Often he was cruel. Our feet and legs were to be exact, precise, and sharp as algorithms, our arms never wooden but supple, fluid extensions of our body. Even from our faces he demanded expression; he was as wont to stop our exercises for a girl's blank stare as for a poorly extended leg. He would draft for us impossible and impossibly long *rond de jambe* combinations, testing our minds as well as our bodies. When poor Francine, who struggled in all of her classes, forgot the combination one time too many, Christian clapped his hands sharply. It was the sound of terror. The piano ceased. He admonished her: "What is wrong with you? You are a terrible dancer, you have a terrible body, and now you have a terrible mind." The class hushed. We watched, paralyzed with fright, as Francine struggled in silence to recreate the combination correctly. Finally, after a long minute, she accomplished this to his satisfaction, and we returned to our bar work together, none as humiliated as our friend but each nearly as determined to remember. In this way, week after week, we grew strong. We trained our bodies to do our will. We learned to dance and to think, to inhabit body and mind together. To this day I can recall that unexpected touch, that first erotic imprint that had nothing to do with sex.

Many years later I learned to be partnered. I learned to give myself over to lifts, to surrender to the form of another body and work with limbs alongside, underneath my own. I let myself be airborne with another, and in those steps for two I understood the gorgeous responsibility of the step that could not be danced alone.

In my last year of graduate school I traveled to Los Angeles to celebrate the thirtieth birthday of my friend Melissa. On Sunday morning, after a late, sunny brunch, Melissa announced we were going dancing.

"They're teaching Lindy Hop," she said.

"What's that?" I asked, as we rose from the table. "What should I wear?"

"I have no idea," she said.

A few hours later we stood among a crowd of awkward women and even more awkward men. Before us stood a glamorous couple. The woman was tall and leggy, with an enormous bosom and platinum hair swept up in perfect rolls and ribbons. She wore a fitted brown skirt with kick pleats that gave a generous view of the broad vintage garters securing her stockings. The man was tall, easily over six feet, and handsome in his gabardine shirt and woolen trousers.

They separated the men and women, then taught us the footwork and led us through basic partnering techniques. My vintage sundress was about three decades removed from the appropriate vintage era. My chic platform shoes were terribly clunky and far too stiff for dancing. Try as I might, I just could not understand what to do. I had no idea what the strange, syncopated triple steps meant or how our part was to match up with the men's. Who had ever heard of a basic step that was eight counts long? The last person I rotated to was Kory. He wore a fitted green t-shirt. He looked like an athlete (and therefore was utterly unlike any boyfriend I had ever had). He had a quiet smile and made polite small talk. He knew how to dance.

After, Melissa and I stood on the edge of the dance floor and sipped our drinks, watching the band and the dancers. From time to time Kory joined us and chatted. When a jam circle broke out, he drew me over to watch. Couple after couple entered the circle. The men wore pleated trousers, gabardine shirts, white bucks. The women wore rayon dresses, pleated skirts, and cashmere sweaters. On their feet were blue oxfords, vintage red wedge soled shoes. Flowers adorned their hair. Their skirts switched as their hips swiveled low and sexy, and they flew in circles around their partners. They Lindy Hopped, legs pumping, heads thrown back. Some Charlestoned, some held each other close and danced a fast, romantic Balboa, quick feet tapping out ever more complicated steps, turns, and dramatic slides across the floor. I didn't fall in love with my husband that night. But I did fall in love with the dance.

Two weeks later Melissa emailed: "That guy Kory called. He's coming to San Francisco and wants you to call him." He wanted to dance.

The winter I was pregnant, Kory and I spent much of our time, as we always had, sprawled on the floor in front of the stereo searching for music to dance to, music to listen to, music to teach to, music for a new routine. We'd follow a few bars of Louis Jordan or Artie Shaw, or Kory would walk through a few steps, pretending to partner me and counting in his head, and I'd nod or suggest a trick I really liked. Pregnancy had not slowed down my dancing at all, and we were still social dancing and teaching several nights a week, though the performing had stopped. Aside from a self-imposed ban on aerials, I could dance just as fast and just as long as I always had, the only difference being that every week my partners, Kory included, had to get used to my expanding girth, and most of my vintage clothes no longer fit.

We had an obsessive habit of watching old video clips of dancers: short, grainy excerpts copied from old movies and edited together into compilations to which we gave names like "SwingTime," or "Hellzapoppin + Early Frankie," or "Hollywood Style + Ella Mae Morse." Some of our clips were very rare, pirated from a university's film archive with a handheld camera by an enterprising and preternaturally talented swing dancer. We watched these clips like people now listen to their iPods—repeatedly, obsessively. We watched and rewound and watched again in slow motion. We stole their moves and invented new ones.

In these moments of stillness the baby erupted into life with a roiling, bubbling motion. "It's like she's dancing," Kory said, which was both obvious and true. Other times I felt a clear, swift kick; sometimes a long, slow roll around the entire circumference of my middle. It was both odd and comforting, having this companion to carry around, signaling to me in her own private Morse code. Although nothing quite equaled the visions of the sonogram to confirm the fact of her existence and its thrills, the quickening was more intimate, a more concrete guarantee of her being.

It was very simple: dead things don't move.

Things that are alive do move, and now she was moving, moving, moving, all the time. By the fourth month Kory could feel her, too, and we both could see evidence of her, not just in the bump of my belly but in its frequent contortions. It was easy for both of us to see and to feel and, therefore, to know that I was no longer singular. I was two. We were three.

As early as the seventh week of pregnancy, a fetus will move in a twitching sort of way. By nine weeks of age the fetus can move its limbs, and as the weeks progress it develops muscle tone, coordination, and strength. There is a distinct sequence to this development: first legs, then arms, then trunk. Until around thirty-two weeks the fetus is uncoordinated. It moves relatively slowly, with writhing or twisting or flailing or flapping motions. To me it often felt like a frenetic, boiling cauldron in my belly. Around the thirty-third week the movements become more coordinated and complex. Then a fetus seems to kick deliberately, to punch and roll in one smooth motion. She will stretch with apparent confidence, almost as if consciously and maliciously sticking a heel into the mother's bladder or under her ribs. Some ultrasounds show babies sucking their thumbs. Increasingly, the fetus can turn her head, move her hands, control her limbs. If you poke her, she might poke back.

In February the winter darkness broke. The sky stretched blue over the Pacific, and the chill evaporated. My spirits, cramped for so many weeks by the fog and rain, lifted. I ate lunch at the beach, watching green waves and sand. As if realizing that spring had come, the baby kicked and shuddered and stretched herself wide across my middle, as if she too were taking in that broad horizon.

By early March her dance was strange and uncontrollable, welcome and unwelcome. I loved it and hated it. Most evenings we watched my swollen belly come alive with kicks, prods, and pokes, as if she were trying to escape. The physical fact of her, marked day after day by her incessant motion—that was what made her real. That was what reminded me that soon enough she would be outside my body. She would be uncontained and probably uncontainable. She would be mine. I was never quite sure which was more frightening: to see my body so miraculously distended or to know that a child was about to dance its way into my life.

She moved on her own time. When I was most still, she was most active: at dawn, in the late afternoon dusk, just before midnight. There were sudden moments of surprise—a sigh, a hiccup, a small adjustment of leg or neck. A lodging of her head against my rib, a limb beneath my hip. There were small flutterings throughout the day, like the susurrus of a flock of settling gulls.

Near the end she grew stronger, her movements more purposeful, and I was often startled by her forcefulness. I imagined her pressing into her dark world, an explorer discovering a continent. I imagined her trying to carve her way out, seeking ever more space. A punching heel, the tickling of tiny fingers, the thrust of the knee. An elbow swells, a knee forms a small hillock. My belly rose in hills and sharp peaks, undulating waves, and, one night, what might have been a forearm or a shin rose to form a small ridge. I felt like a world, with a world inside me.

Our bodies remember so that we may forget. The thing called muscle memory, a knowledge that resides deep in the bones, comes only with repetition, with endless hours of practice. It is experiential knowledge, shared by all who work with their bodies, and it is a knowledge that precedes language and thought. It allows the body to know what to do before it is told. Only then, in that surrendered knowledge, can your body truly be said to know something, to know anything. It is this knowledge that possesses the batter at the moment of the swing, the diver as she opens to pierce the water, the dancer as she unfurls, alive and jubilant, from a pirouette. It is knowledge shared by the child who catches her balance, and the baby who has learned, finally, to sit or crawl.

What I remember: inhabiting my body. Understanding how space unfolds from within. How power begins there, coiled in darkness, then is loosed, translated to torso, to limbs, and beyond to the world. I learned the expanse of my body, I learned my body's limits.

Our first movements are buried in darkness. The womb is the center of our first world, a globe curving to meet our shape. Unconscious we test the waters. We roll against our horizon and kick to the very limits of our universe. Shadow boxers, we imprint our own geography, an embryonic Braille on our mother's body. Long before we are seen or heard, we are felt. Before we cry or think or love, before we breathe or know or speak, we move. Bodies do many things, in many ways. But first, they move.

MY PHANTOM SELF

It began in February, in my twenty-third week. It felt like a bruise, a small nob of tenderness lodged deep inside me, just to the left of my tailbone.

On my daily walk along the beach the dull ache metamorphosized. With electric quickness the pain shot through my hip so four blocks early, I turned home. For several paces I felt nothing and then, without warning, a hot flash at the base of my spine. My left leg recoiled from the ground. The pain receded, and I slowly resumed walking, attending carefully to my posture and gait. For several paces I felt nothing. Then, another flash of pain and my leg crumpled beneath me. Somehow, I limped home.

That evening, I hobbled from kitchen to couch. The slightest pressure on my left side brought tears to my eyes. Within twenty-four hours I could no longer walk.

There are two sciatic nerves, both of which run along the base of the spine, through the pelvis, down the back of the leg, to the foot, forming a kind of lancet arch. They are the largest nerves in the body and their inflammation is not uncommon in pregnancy, although sciatica does exist more generally in the so-called normal population.

For twenty-three weeks I had felt strong and fit, and mostly happy. I had walked, practiced yoga, danced until midnight. Then sciatica arrived. Daily it worsened. By the third day, it was a constant presence, an unwelcome, nasty lodger. To bend, to lift, to walk was excruciating. Mornings, I lay in bed for forty-five minutes after waking, too afraid of the pain to rise. Kory opened the sofa bed in the living room, and I spent my evenings supine. He brought me ice packs and hot water bottles, tucked in mountains of supporting pillows, and I lay there like a perverse Cleopatra, pampered, in pain.

Not long after, I discovered that many pregnant women don't sleep with their husbands anyway. A friend taught me how to construct a fort of pillows to support my back and hips. Her own fort had driven her husband out of their bed weeks before, and although her own sciatica had long since disappeared, he continued to sleep in the spare room with the new feather pillows provided by his mother-in-law. My friend was buoyed by the surreptitious questioning of an eight-month pregnant colleague: Do you still sleep with your husband? Around my own column of pillows and rolled blankets, precious little room was left for Kory. As he climbed into his ever-narrowing sliver of bed, he eyed me worriedly. "You're not going to kick me out of bed, are you?"

Still as a corpse, I approximated comfort. But whenever I tried to rise, I found inactivity had seized the nerve and froze my hip like a rusty hinge. Using Kory as a crutch, I limped down the short hallway, my breath racing. Unable to bend at the waist, it took many minutes to wash my face. Kory supported me until I reached the edge of the bed, then watched helplessly as I began the slow process of lying down. (Although I could not have gotten by without him, there was a certain extraneousness to his presence. There was nothing he could do to help me or to ease my pain. This was another metaphor, though I did not realize it at the time.) First, I stood by the side of the bed and stared at it for a long time. Kory couldn't lift me because no matter how slow or gentle he was, the pain required to fold my body into his arms was unbearable. So I took another minute to steel my nerves. Since I couldn't bend at the waist without searing, flashing pain, climbing into bed on my hands and knees was just as miserable as sitting and sliding slowly down on my side. Finally I began the terrible process of lowering myself down. Most nights, I attempted to induce a kind of paralysis of the hip, then, inch by inch, lay myself down. Finally flat on my back, I cried. Sleep came slow in that funereal position.

One morning I called my mother in New Jersey: "What if I have this and have to go through labor?"

"That's when you ask for drugs," she said.

Sciatica is listed as a common complaint of pregnancy in every advice book on the market. Most usually the result of a slipped disk, no one knows for sure what causes it in pregnancy. Some practitioners have theorized its relation to the pressure of the growing uterus on the sciatic nerve, or to the postural changes often called the "pride of pregnancy," or to the baby's position (although my perinatologist assured me that there is no proven link between this and sciatic pain). Sometimes it goes away on its own, he said. Other times it doesn't. Sometimes it gets worse. Other times it doesn't. In the general population, acupuncture can help eliminate the pain, but the pressure points that treat the inflammation can also induce labor. Once pregnant and in sciatic pain, there is little you can do to get rid of it. I was advised to try ice and heat therapy. Massage. Yoga. Rest.

Twice a week I still mustered a trip to yoga class. Though I was barely able to maneuver the gently sloping hill that led to the studio, the poses were surprisingly benign. Downward and upward cat, downward dog, half-dog at the wall, tailor's pose, pigeon pose. All offered some relief and a few gave an extraordinary release, an expansion in my sacral region that was the physical equivalent of light. Between the poses I could barely move, and my friends adjusted my sticky mat, brought me blocks and bolsters, unfolded my chair. But the poses themselves were miraculous, like tiny blessings. Each class I longed for the one saving pose that would realign my body, emancipate me from the pain which was far worse than any I had ever sustained. Broken bones had throbbed and pulsed, then been immobilized in plaster. Sprains ached but diminished daily. Even a burn could be cooled, salved, and covered. But this pain was hot and deep and total. It affected every movement I made. Bending for a dropped pencil, lifting a small stack of books, twisting for a lamp switch, or placing any weight at all on my left foot invoked a pain as raw as it was malignant. Most nights, simply turning over in bed proved beyond me.

Until the middle of the twentieth century, the modern view of pain was relatively straightforward: the experience of pain was considered a simple, sensory phenomenon predicated on a one-way movement of cause and effect. A boy throws a punch at you and your arm throbs. The paper cuts your finger, the slice stings. Labor begins and your body convulses. While the degree of injury might determine the quality of the pain, the model was basically a mechanistic one, its fundamental premise unchanged since it had been articulated by René Descartes in the seventeenth century.

In Descartes' model, pain functions something like a toppling row of dominoes. External stimuli activate peripheral nerve ends, which in turn displace central nerve ends, which in turn rearrange the flow of "animal spirits" to initiate a physical, reflexive response. The theory was illustrated by a large half-naked baby sitting erect beside a burning wood fire, his hand extended boldly over the flames. He is about to touch the fire, recoil in pain, and learn that fire is hot and will hurt him. But Descartes' point was that the child will react to pain before his mind knows pain. Fundamentally, Descartes' body functioned as a machine. It might have been a machine with a soul and a mind but it had the capacity to function independently of these, on a kind of biological autopilot.

Of course, from one perspective this model of pain is enlightened, for it suggests that pain is not, as the Puritans believed, proof of one's wickedness. Nor is it a spiritual trial to be borne on the path to salvation, or even the means to earning such salvation. After Descartes it was inevitable that pain would be emptied of spiritual meaning. (Though not, perhaps, of spiritual value.) By the middle of the twentieth century, however, some doctors had begun to suspect that pain was neither transparent nor even purely physical. Henry Knowles Beecher noticed that soldiers injured on the front lines in World War II tended to complain much less of their wounds than did his post-operative civilian patients back in Massachusetts. He wrote: "Strong emotion can block pain. That is common experience." Beecher and Raymond W. Houde, who worked at Memorial Sloan-Kettering Cancer Center, found that pain has a subjective component: a patient's perception of his own pain is a crucial aspect of diagnosis and evaluation. It became understood that pain functions as more than a purely mechanical system; it involves states of mind, even one's own subjectivity.

Then, in 1965, the thinking about pain changed. Troubled by the problem of phantom limb pain, which clearly could not be attributed to external damage to the afflicted body part (since said body part did not exist), psychologist Ronald Melzack and physiologist Patrick D. Wall collaborated to propose Gate Control Theory, which revolutionized the study and understanding of pain. Considered by some to be the most influential paper on pain ever written, "Pain Mechanisms: A New Theory" proposed that a gating mechanism located in the spinal cord controls the flow of nerve impulses between the body and the brain. While these gates might be opened by "noxious stimuli"— the slow impulses of pain pounding at the door like a horde of barbarians—they might also be closed by impulses from the brain. That is, the brain might send signals to the gate to not let the intruder through, or maybe to let through only one, or three. In other words, pain moves neither inevitably nor directly from the site of the injury to the brain but is modulated by these gates. To see how this works practically, try applying ice indirectly to your next injury. To be effective as an analgesic, ice needs only to rest somewhere on the nerve between the injury and the brain.

Pain, then, became a complex, layered phenomenon, entailing physiological, psychological, emotional, and subjective aspects of the self. At the center of this new understanding of pain was not the child's burned hand but the child's brain. This did not mean, of course, that a person's pain might be "in her head"—as in fictive, spurious, or psychosomatic—but only that the way one experiences pain does not necessarily correlate directly with the degree or even with the quality of the physiological injury. In fact, one of the most startling things that the Melzack and Wall theory suggested was that all pains are not created equal.

It is fitting that in pregnancy one experiences pain differently. The changes that begin in your body have profound effects if not on your brain, then certainly on your mind. When my body morphed to accommodate the cell, the blastocyst, the fetus, so, too, did my mind alter its understanding of the body that was attached to it.

Throughout pregnancy, many women experience the painful physical manifestations of change as Otherness: sore abdominal muscles, aching hips and shoulders, nausea, nosebleeds. I understood these phenomena as phenomena, not as part of any body I had ever known. In pregnancy the painful things that happened to my body seemed to happen upon me, and the afflicted part was not exactly a part of me—at least not in the same way it was before the baby began to grow. Very often my mind would rise above my self to proclaim: This misery is temporary, a side effect of that thing inside me. The truth was, I had been changed and I would never again be quite the same person I had been before, neither in mind nor in body. Some days I took comfort in the fact that even if I was miserable, the baby, at least, was oblivious to my discomfort.

Even when pain is not immediately present to remind you of what your body is going through, there is hardly an aspect of the maternal body that is unaffected by pregnancy. Systemic and physiological changes alter radically how the pregnant body works and how it feels. While most of these changes are relatively benign and borne in good stead by most women, they can also cause odd and distinct discomforts. In the earliest weeks of pregnancy the hormone relaxin, manufactured initially by the corpus luteum surrounding the egg and eventually by the placenta, floods the mother's body, loosening her ligaments like well-used elastic, spreading her joints, widening her pelvis to accommodate the baby. Some days relaxin feels like a kind of torture, a hormonal rack that makes every joint of your body vulnerable. Knees give out, shoulders ache, fingers and neck feel slightly unhinged.

Because of the increased production of estrogen and progesterone, breasts feel sore and ponderously heavy, sometimes for weeks or months. Some pregnant women find their contact lenses irritating or discover their eyeglass prescription has changed because corneas become 3 percent thicker and the eyeball fluid pressure can decrease. Increased levels of phosphorus or decreased levels of calcium cause painful leg cramps. Nasal cavities swell, mucus production increases. In my second trimester I would find myself unable to breathe through my nose whenever I lay down. For hours each night I sat in the dark, sipping hot tea and reading by a small, honey-colored lamp, while Kory slumbered beside me. Then one day I began to sneeze. These were not the relief-granting single sneezes that occasionally seized me during normal life, but fleets of sneezes that came quick and hard and made my throat hurt and my eyes water; they disrupted rather than relieved, and if they overtook me while driving, I had to pull my car to the side of the road.

Under the influence of fetal and placental hormones, a pregnant woman's skin may feel greasy, pigmentation may alter, hair may grow more abundantly (and in unwanted places like the chin, upper lip, or cheeks). These same hormones cause digestion to slow down and the esophagus to relax, resulting in heartburn and constipation. Increased blood flow to all tissues may cause gums to become unusually sore and bleed easily. Other vascular changes can result in varicose veins or painful hemorrhoids. Such varicosities are caused by the growing uterus, which can impede or block the passage of blood back to the heart. Under its pressure, veins swell and dilate. As the growing belly stretches the skin, it may itch interminably, as mine did, or develop stretch marks. As the baby grows, it literally rearranges your internal organs, causing mechanical changes, like the shallow breathing that results when the baby pushes against the diaphragm.

My pregnant friends and I spoke about our bodies with a certain loving detachment. We compared our dizziness, our hunger, our heartburn, our growing midlines as if they were data in an experiment conducted by some distant, irrational scientist, rather than our own daily symptoms. "My gut feels like I've done five hundred crunches" . . . "I can't sleep" . . . "I can't sleep either" . . . "I'm still nauseous" . . . "I have carpal tunnel syndrome" . . . "I'm congested" . . . "My hips ache" . . . "I was up from one until five" . . . "I have leg cramps in the middle of the night" . . . "I sneeze all day" . . . "My skin is blotchy" . . .

"My skin is oily" . . . "I'm exhausted" . . . "The baby's leg is stuck under my rib."

Most of the time we laughed and carried on. Our bodies had become uncanny, unwieldy things. Alien things. Deeply intimate things. They were changing, self-directing vessels. They had knowledge and being and function independent of us. And while it is surely true that our bodies work without us every day of our lives, pregnancy throws this captivity of the self into high relief.

My sciatic pain was an obvious reminder of pregnancy, a remainder of the body's gravid change. Yet it also reminded me that my body was not exactly mine. It belonged now to the pregnancy. Eventually it would be overtaken by labor. In nursing I would hand it over to my child. Someday my body would appear to be returned to me, but it would, finally, be covered over in death. There was only so much I could do to manage the plodding biology of mortality. Certainly, I could keep myself healthy, safe, sustained. But on some fundamental level things were quite out of my control. So, as the sciatica refused to abate, I began to wonder just how much of my body had ever really been "mine" to begin with. This was not simply a spiritual, philosophical question—although it was certainly that—but a pragmatic, biological one.

Most days, we like to think there is contiguity between ourselves and our bodies, that the two are one. It is no longer in vogue to wallow in the morass of Cartesian dualism. We say, "I think, therefore I am," and experience little terror about the division between the "I" that thinks and the "I" that is thought about. Postmodern subjects that we are, we know that the "I" that thinks is as much a construct as the body that is thought about. However, commonsensically and perhaps more significantly for many of us, most of the time there simply is no dilemma: the body is as much a part of "me" as the mind.

Pregnant and in pain, it felt much easier to sunder the duality. I preferred to understand that I inhabited rather than possessed my body. Pregnancy had established an uneasy coexistence between what I understood as my self and what I experienced as my body. Like a lame duck, my body was accountable to me only by the slimmest of margins. It was, perhaps, the opposite of someone with a phantom limb, an irrevocably missing arm, or leg, or hand that still belongs to its owner. My body was no phantom, but I no longer understood it as mine. My body was precisely the thing that reminded me, day after day, minute upon minute, of what had been lost.

Ronald Melzack believes there is a deep structure in the brain, an anatomical substrate of identity that enables us to think of ourselves as whole. A large and widespread network of neurons, this structure loops between various areas of the brain, processing and synthesizing neuronal impulses. As the loops diverge and converge, areas of the brain may interact or they may work in splendid, tandem isolation. Impulses travel this network like so many runaway cars on a roller coaster, coupling here, separating there, creating our sense of self, our sense of ourselves as one. We experience not a multitude of discrete and disparate sensations (here an arm, here a head, there the ground beneath our feet, here—on that arm—another's touch), but we understand a single person, a cohering at the center of our experience. We gather a distinct, original point of view. Melzack calls this structure the neuromatrix, from matrix, from the Latin *matr-*, *mater-*, meaning *womb*.

A matrix is a lovely, complex thing. It is, on the one hand, a generative space, a maternal, gestating space of origin from which, out of darkness and blankness, something new—a sense of self—might emerge. It is a creative space, too, a place that writes itself on the newness. Like the bronze cast out of the negative mold, what is borne from the matrix will always bear its form and its signature.

So, too, in its endless looping, processing, and synthesizing, the neuromatrix writes itself on the body, producing a neuro-signature out of that never ending "stream of awareness." We read, as it were, our body's secret neuronal language and we recognize our self. Built in, genetically determined and capable of being modified by experience, the "neurosignature" is a pliable but constant thing, a voice singing ever more difficult notes, an ever-expanding poem, a song of the self that has no end.

When I felt pain, then, I was not feeling something that occurred outside of myself. There was no external equivalent to the throbbing, stabbing, or grinding pain I felt in my back. Outside of me, the pain simply did not exist. Melzack would argue that my brain (like all other brains) was built to produce these sensations. An injury like my sciatica, for instance, might seem to occur "out there" in my body, but the quality of the experience—how it feels to be in pain—can only be generated internally by the brain. Phantom limbs become comprehensible, Melzack theorizes, because "the brain generates the experience of the body." The brain tells the body: *There is the arm, the arm hurts.* It does not matter that the arm is not there as long as the brain thinks it is. Melzack concludes that external events—sustaining an injury or losing a limb—can only modulate experience, not create it. As it generates the experience of the body, the brain, like the mythical phoenix, seeks always a return to wholeness.

My pregnant body was more than whole. It was, in fact, two. In the matrix of my womb I was generating my daughter, and as she loosed her never-ending stream of hormones, she flooded my never-ending stream of awareness. I felt so much myself and yet not myself, because I was and I wasn't. Perhaps my brain understood this. As it looped and processed and synthesized those familiar, pedestrian impulses of the Self, there was an Other there, too, a roadblock, a detour, a lovely unexpected vista opening where none had been before. Already my daughter had begun to write her Self onto my Self, and I had been irretrievably altered. There, in the dark, she had signed herself, her signature a shadowy palimpsest, here and there visible, here and there vanishing beneath my own.

Two weeks after it began, the sciatica disappeared. I was resting in bed, hot water bottle on my rump, breathing in a few calm moments during a brief respite from the pain. The baby kicked a little, and then began a slow, sure somersault that rippled from the bottom of my belly to the top. It felt like an elevator rising slowly through my middle. In five seconds the movement had passed; three hours later the sciatica was gone. The next morning I lay in bed, in sunlight. I could roll and twist. I could touch my husband and bear to be touched. I rose from bed and felt I had already given birth.

Whether she turned or twisted or rolled or lifted, I will never know. But I begged her never again to cause me such pain. It was a futile request.

The pain had been real enough, but it passed quickly into the realm of metaphor. The conventional reading of Eve's curse rightly conjures the pain of labor: "I will intensify the pangs of your childbearing; in pain shall you bring forth children." The pain of labor so terrified me that most of the time I chose not to think of it at all. Yet there had been great pain before labor. Certainly there would be pain after. Even then, so long before her birth, I knew that the pain of my child was bound to become my own. Her fevers, scrapes, and chills would be written on my body. Her heartaches, confusions, and devastations generated in my soul, too. Though my womb would mold her and cast her out, my altered self would cling to her, remembering her shadowy presence like a poem learned by heart. After, my pain would surely be doubled. If pain was a condition of this pregnancy, it was only because it was a condition of life. Lurking in my future was a pain so formidable that I knew one day, being unable to walk might well seem the easier burden.

SONG OF
THE SELF

One Monday night in February, three days before Valentine's Day, my husband came home from work and announced, "I wrote a song today." I regarded him skeptically and returned to fixing dinner.

I had often known my husband to sing spontaneously. When we were dating he sometimes serenaded me, usually in the car. It was a surprise to me, and it seemed a felicitous talent because I can't sing at all. In fact, no one in my family can carry a tune, in spite of the fact that we all frequently try.

Since our marriage, I had only eavesdropped on this private pleasure. Sometimes I caught him singing along with the radio, or singing as he made waffles, or singing in the proverbial shower. Sometimes he sang to himself for no reason at all. I had stumbled upon him humming a tune the same way other wives might overhear an angry muttering. Usually he sang old-time crooner songs, Sinatra or Cole Porter, or sometimes, if he was feeling feisty, he'd break out an obscure rock-a-billy beat or some early Elvis. He sang with a rich, mellow voice that I enjoyed, and he sang carefully, as if he were thinking about each note. He had a habit of phrasing that suggested he lived inside the song, as though he knew what the lyrics meant to him and what he wanted them to mean for me, or for whoever happened not to be listening at the moment. I knew, too, that he had an enormous lyrical repertoire that he could retrieve spontaneously, much as an evangelist might summon Leviticus, chapter and verse, to punctuate his jeremiad. On long car trips between San Francisco and Los Angeles, when the only radio signal strong enough for our old tuner was beamed from the oldies station, Kory could sing along for hours and never miss a word. He seemed to know the songbook to every Broadway musical ever staged and had passing familiarity with most of what Ella Fitzgerald recorded before 1945. He remembered the hits and obscuriania of his high school and college days (and of my high school and college days, too), every Elvis hit, fifties pop, sixties surf rock, seventies ballad, the requisite sub-pop, anything by Sam Cooke. He could even hum the soundtrack to many of his favorite movies, a skill he acquired as a young child. His mother recalls him turning to her once, around age six, and humming a tune, then asking, "Do you remember the part of the movie where the music went like this?"

I loved this musical part of him because it impressed and delighted me, but also because the facts of what he knew were so old-fashioned. My husband had a streak of personality that belonged to another era, and it seemed to me a good thing that a dad would know the lyrics to *Oklahoma!* or could teach the kid something about Nat King Cole.

Yet even though very early in our relationship I had come to accept his superiority in this realm, I had never known him to write songs. As far as I was concerned, his musical talent was purely imitative. Apparently I knew little about the secret ways of my husband. Unbeknownst to me he had cultivated a habit of writing Cole Porter–esque tunes on his drive to work. It began when he was making the fifty-minute commute in an old Ford truck with no radio. To combat the boredom, he told himself stories. Out loud. These were not the quiet musings, silent fantasies, or even the stupendous what-ifs that most of us tell ourselves. We all tell ourselves narratives about fame and glory and new-found career satisfaction. We're all captivated by private, selfish daydreams. No, Kory's stories were fully voiced, fully animated adventures. They spilled out in a wonderful babble as his characters engaged, did battle, reconciled. They threw out witty asides. Soon I discovered that this Homeric compulsion was fundamental to his character. While he is usually the quietest person in the room at a social event, in private he is downright garrulous. Within the safe confines of his truck he invented plots, held long conversations between characters, and narrated exploits with dramatic flair. In one two-week period he perfected the voices of the entire cast of characters for a short film. I was rarely privy to these voices, and then only after an especially good dinner with an especially nice bottle of wine. When I first heard these voices I sat transfixed, watching my husband perform a character-filled scene complete with rising, falling, and climaxing action, with pitch-perfect voices. At first, I didn't know what to make of it. In thirty-six years I had spoken aloud to myself exactly twice. Both times I was studying for my doctoral exams and both involved the recitation of Whitman poems. My husband, on the other hand, seemed possessed by a host of demons. Years later his talent was confirmed for me by our mutual friend, who had worked as a voice actor before finding his true calling as a master sommelier. Paul readily admitted that Kory could do more, and better, voices. Kory's only problem, said Paul, was that he would do them neither on command nor in public. Thus I accepted Kory's talent and filed it away with his singing, something I loved about him that was also slightly strange.

Over the years I had known exceptions to Kory's reserve, like the Halloween when he astounded his office by winning the office costume party. This was no small feat at the gaming company where he worked as a development artist. Most of the company dressed up for the holiday, and most had been planning their costumes for months. When you put together a group of creative, tech-minded gaming geeks—most of whom are single, or at least childless, and who work long hours conjuring up virtual worlds peopled with Miltonian characters engaged in epic battles for the fate of the undead—well, you can imagine the implications for Halloween.

That year Kory arrived at work wearing an unassuming pair of black snowboarding pants, a polyester *Star Trek* shirt, and a pair of thick-rimmed eyeglasses broken at the bridge and poorly repaired with masking tape. One prominent blemish was pasted on the side of his nose. Of course, a Trekkie is a relatively unoriginal Halloween getup, standard fare, really, among his crowd. However, in addition to the costume, my husband had also assumed a character. On a white nametag, proudly displayed above the *Enterprise* insignia on the left chest, he had crossed out "Ensign" and written in "Capt." And thus he remained until the close of business that day: an earnest, beleaguered devotee of the *Enterprise*, consumed by the meticulous fiction of Trekkie science. As he tells it, his coworkers were gathered around his terminal all day, asking the ~~Ensign~~\captain questions:

"Why do you love *Star Trek*?"

"Because its vision of the future is utopian. Everything there keeps getting better."

"Who is your favorite character?"

"Commander William Riker, second in command on TNG. That's *The Next Generation* to you."

"Why is he your favorite?"

"Because we have a lot in common. Both our dads left us when we were little."

"What is your favorite movie?

"*First Contact.* Because Richard Frakes directed it and acted in it."

"Where's your phaser?"

"My mom doesn't like me to have guns. I told her I could put it on stun, but that didn't convince her."

Kory had told me nothing of his plan. I learned of it that evening, when he related the accomplishment that had won him a coveted gift certificate to Toys "R" Us®. The fact that the prize was so coveted (Toys "R" Us® had a large supply of action figures, which apparently figured prominently in his office) was another thing I didn't know about him. I imagine he won the contest not just for his role playing but because it was so unexpected.

After two years of marriage I was still getting used to the depth of my husband's *hilaritus*, the Greek virtue that derives from the combination of wit and quick thinking. In him it would emerge suddenly, a transformation as surprising as a sleight of hand. Though I believed I was looking at one man, I would suddenly be compelled by another who had taken his place. The effect was not unlike seeing the alternating figures of an optical illusion, the vase that resolves itself into two profiles and then, ghostlike, shimmers back into view. Year after year, knowing my husband involved a similar adjustment of perspective, the same deepening of vision, the subsequent readjustment of my point of view. I knew, for instance, that Kory had no sense of time and that he would always take longer and be later than he said he would be. I knew that he could remember names and dates from decades past and obscure facts about dinosaurs and film but that he would forget to fax the medical forms unless I asked him three times. I knew that he would easily forget to eat, that he loved the future in all its forms, and that he would always be the optimistic one. He hated asparagus, beets, and eggplant (all otherworldly vegetables to him) and loved sugar especially German chocolate cake (something I still do not understand).

He would kiss me good-bye every morning no matter how sleepy or grumpy I was, and bring me coffee in bed no matter how pressed for time he might be. These things were predictable, the routine blessings and negotiations that ground every marriage. These were the things that I loved. Other things annoyed me, but those I tried to accept because they were also my husband. Ralph Waldo Emerson wrote, just before the middle of the nineteenth century, that "we pass for what we are." We can read character like an acrostic, he argued, but "forward, backward, or across, it still spells the same thing." Marriage had taught me that loving Kory meant I could not ignore the parts that I wished weren't there even though it meant I would almost always have to pay the bills, remind him to get a haircut, and every spring wish that he would change his mind about asparagus.

As much as I had come to know about him, however, there were still days when Kory would surprise me with the perfect gift—a fountain pen and red leather journal, for instance, or a wireless keyboard that I didn't know I wanted—or a song, or an escapade that emerged from a life utterly mysterious and foreign. In the first months of our courtship, our differences were a source of constant scrutiny for me. Almost seven years his senior, I was finishing a Ph.D. in English and he had never finished his B.A. We were raised on opposite coasts. I had migrated, over the course of a decade, from New Jersey to England, Northern Ireland, Holland, Paris, Dublin, New York, and Texas, finally settling in California. He had traveled all over the United States and to Japan and China but had never lived outside California. I had been granted, with my doctorate, a designated emphasis in feminist theory. He had dated women with fake breasts. All my friends were artists, writers, or academics. He worked in the animation industry which, at the time, I did not consider art. I read Wallace Stevens; he read Stephen King. Once, when I sent him an Emily Dickinson poem, he thought the stanzaic breaks delineated two different poems. Eventually I decided some of these things didn't matter. The fake breasts, for instance, or the inability to read Dickinson. Other things I decided to learn about because he was sexy and surprisingly kind. Today he knows something about Hemingway and I can find sublimity in *The Iron Giant*. We both love good children's books, old movies, talk radio. We can go to museums together and eat happily in any city in the world. We can jitterbug all night long.

It is easy to think that you know someone: a friend, a parent, a sibling, a lover. We expect certain behaviors—or, at least, a known range of behavior—from those we love. We think we know our spouse's mind, can describe our friends' traits, tolerate our parents' eccentricities. We are guided by what we understand, consciously or unconsciously, to be the "certainty" of the self. More Emerson's students than we realize, we ground ourselves in the sacredness of character: "Trust thyself: every heart vibrates to that iron string." We trust others in this same way. We may not expect consistency from them, that most distressing of hobgoblins, but we implicitly understand Emerson's supposition that "no man can violate his nature." We go through life largely assured of the certainty of the Other we love, secure in our knowledge of him or her. If we are to love truly and consistently, we finally come to understand another of Emerson's claims: character teaches above our wills. Whatever we might want from a lover—whoever we might want him or her to be— willing it thus will not make it so. What we want has little bearing on what the other person actually is.

Which is why, in love there will always be surprise. For even— and maybe especially—in love, there remains a part of the other that is inaccessible. Poets have long understood this. Rainer Maria Rilke likened love to two solitudes, bordering and protecting each other. Walt Whitman, that poet of great, omnivorous sympathies and mergings, warns:

Whoever you are holding me now in hand,
Without one thing all will be useless,
I give you fair warning before you attempt me further,
I am not what you supposed, but far different.

Even Elizabeth Bishop, writing of knowledge more generally,
declaims:

It is like what we imagine knowledge to be:
dark, salt, clear, moving, utterly free,
drawn from the cold hard mouth
of the world, derived from the rocky breasts
forever, flowing and drawn, and since
our knowledge is historical, flowing and flown.

We cannot fully know the other whom we love. Nor, perhaps, should we even desire this knowledge. For in the gap, in
that flowing void of knowledge, desire is cultivated and love
blooms. We must have the illusion and security of knowledge,
but we must also have the mystery that creates longing and
desire. There will always be parts of our selves that we hold
apart, and there will always be places in our lovers that remain
veiled. To love truly is not simply to know; it is also to accept
not knowing.

I knew it would be no different with our daughter, who was
about to become a welcome stranger in our home. In those
pregnant, expectant months, we knew little about her, aside
from her gender, and something about how and when she
moved. Soon we would know what she looked like. We would
know the curve of her head, the light in her eyes, the grasp of
her small fingers, the addictive softness of her skin. We would
know the strength of her kick, the smell of soap in her babyfine
hair, even the paste of sweat and dirt that hid in the folds of her
neck. We would know how many times a day she fed, how well

she could sleep. We would begin to know her smile and recognize her voice. We would meet her personality, acknowledge her emerging personhood.

These things, too, would change.

What we gathered in the first hours after her birth would certainly evolve in the days, months, years to follow, so that she would become a lesson in caretaking and in joy, but also one in knowledge. We would watch her character forming as rapidly as her body, and in spite of the intimacy that existed between us now—that impossible closeness, her self being subsumed completely in mine—she would soon become separate, an Other like her father, who was to me known and not known. She would be another iron string vibrating, changing the tune of our family. We would know her joys, her sorrows, her talents great and small, what would make her laugh. But, like all children, some part of her—if only a small part—would remain a mystery, divisible and separate. We would someday ask ourselves, as most parents must, Where did she come from? That we would know full well the answer, the deep intimacy in which her life began, only made the question more unnerving.

I imagined Kory had written a limerick, a catchy verse or two, possibly a refrain. I didn't expect much.

"Is it for me?" I asked, mildly curious.

"Sure," he said.

"Is it for Valentine's Day?"

"If you want it to be," he answered.

"Can I hear it?"

"Do you want to hear it?"

"Do you want to sing it for me?"

He shrugged. "I guess so."

"Do you want to wait until Thursday?"

"It doesn't matter," he said.

But of course it did. He sat at the table, still in his coat, and transcribed the lyrics that had been in his head all day. And then, just before dinner, he asked, "Are you ready?"

"Sure," I said.

"Don't look at me," he said. He blushed and hung his head. I laughed. He angled his chair away from me.

"Don't look at me," he repeated. "I get embarrassed when you look at me."

"I won't look."

"I can't sing if you're looking at me."

He lowered his head and took a deep breath. He turned his chair forty-five degrees away from me. He straightened his arms, cleared his throat, and sang, surprising me with melody.

"You take a little bit of sugar,
You take a little bit of spice,
A whole lot of love,
And everything nice,
And what do you get?
Well, I'm gonna tell ya—
You get my Isabella!

"She's got sparkling blue eyes,
And a button for a nose,
Two ticklish feet,
And ten cute little toes,
She's also got the heart
Of this here fella—
There goes my Isabella!

"And in the night when she cries,
The dark purple clouds fill the skies,
But when she laughs and smiles at me,
The sky is blue and the grass is green!

"Well, she sure sounds perfect,
You say she sure sounds great,
If you want her for your girl,
You're a little too late,
Cause on this last fact
I don't have to sell ya,
She's my Isabella!"

First I cried, because I was pregnant and everything made me cry, then I laughed. Then I cried and laughed at once.

"I guess we have to name her Isabella now," I said.

Kory shrugged and said something about the bridge not working, then he shrugged away the formula of the song. I imagined him singing the song to Ella. I thought how lucky she was—not because a simple song was composed for her before she was born, but because she had a father who was inspired by the very idea of her, by everything that he couldn't yet know about her and quite possibly never would.

THE MIND-
BODY PROBLEM

My yoga teacher, Elaine, often told us that pregnancy is a blessed time, a time perfect for meditation because the whole body is turned inward, focused and intent on the life unfolding within. Much of the time I experienced pregnancy as a state of mindless contentment. I was simply happy, and happy to simply conjure small pleasures: making pasta, tending my plants, buying flowers, listening to Ella Mae Morse (because I knew that now the baby could hear). I read and I walked along the ocean. I had long talks with my friends. I descended into domesticity. For the first time I reckoned the value of home, that private space that nineteenth-century women (and men) saw as a retreat from the unhealthy materialism of the public sphere. For them, home provided a counterbalance to work; it was a spiritual and emotional corrective to worldly concerns. The notion of radical domesticity—that the home was a productive, necessary, political space—had always seemed to me to be a neat fiction, a story women and feminist scholars had told themselves in order to explain the gendered division of labor and life that had ruled American culture for centuries. But now it really did seem to me that our home was much more than a retreat from the public, professional lives we led. It seemed to be the very center of life itself. Other things became subordinate, adjunctive to the home that we were creating between the four simple walls of our nondescript apartment. What really mattered in my life seemed to take place not in my professional life, not at the university, nor in my writing, nor in Kory's career, but in those moments when we were together, simply: the cooking, eating, shopping, even the cleaning, the time we took to be with each other, dancing or not dancing, reading or not reading, listening to the radio or not. Unconsciously, my values shifted. What caused me great pleasure changed, and the result was that I found myself generally happier than I had ever known myself to be.

This dumb happiness came not without cost. At times I knew that something odd had happened to my mind. It was not quick like it had once been. It felt less agile, less aware, less searching. Like my body, my mind had become ponderous and consumed by the dailiness of life, by the task of organizing things other than ideas. The real world had begun to consume the imagined one. In my twenty-seventh week I began to understand Elaine's dictum newly: being pregnant is like being in a cocoon. Just as your baby is wrapped in the warmth and darkness of your womb, so are you lost in the haze of hormones that emanates from it. It was not unlike living behind a veil, observing the world from a beautiful but muffled vantage. My best friend called it placenta brain, a term originally coined by midwives.

The experience of pregnancy as an increasingly surreal, altered state was most pronounced at the end of my sixth month. I had begun to crave caffeine again, and when dusk fell I longed to have a cocktail. I grew tired of cottage cheese and protein counts and wearied of my studied diet. This was also around the time that the pregnancy began to show to strangers. While Kory had warm and fuzzy dreams of new baby girls, in my dreams the baby was a mouse, a giant shrimp, a homunculus, an infant who had been taught to talk by her cousins and who berated me for breastfeeding the wrong way. I wondered what had happened to my tiny, helpless baby. In the morning, I could not wait for her to be born. Slowly, I came to accept that I wasn't living in quite the same way that I had ever lived before. Pregnancy may be fundamentally a physical state but the transformation it works on your body is so encompassing that, eventually, it enacts an equivalent psychological and emotional revolution.

While pregnancy's pains are fairly well documented, its pleasures are generally not made quite so public. In order to accommodate the fetus's great need for oxygen, the maternal heart, whose rate increases by 10 to 20 percent, pumps 50 percent more blood (up to one and a half liters more than before pregnancy). Cardiac capacity increases by 40 to 45 percent, and oxygen consumption rises by 20 to 30 percent. These changes have prompted some researchers to suggest that if maternal capacities are maintained through a postpartum exercise routine, pregnancy may actually increase a mother's athletic ability. If pregnant women are moody, anxious, or a little depressed, they can be just as easily possessed by a deep calm. This feeling of contentment and well-being is nearly unobtainable in non-pregnant life. While such possession can make you absent-minded, well, maybe that is the prerogative of being pregnant. In the end I found it to be a relief and a reprieve to accept this shift of psyche. Why not allow myself, for this short time, to be absolved from the daily responsibilities of life? Why not let myself forget? Later I would have to remember everything. And while pregnancy can induce sleeplessness, the dreams fueled by hormonal wash become fantastically, joyously vivid. A secret, nocturnal pleasure is whispered from one gravid woman to the next: more than once I was awoken by orgasm brought on by dream. Sexual pleasure can be heightened, too; it is often more intense, more enduring, more craved, and more welcome. Many of my friends would come to agree, with more than a little nostalgia, that nothing beats pregnant sex.

The sense that so many women have of being physically hijacked, overtaken by the pregnancy for better and not just for worse, is supported by its biological story. Most of us assume that the mother's body takes care of the growing fetus. Research suggests, however, that the fetus and placenta, through a complicated nexus of chemical and hormonal signals, are in fact the ones in control. Together the fetus and placenta regulate the development of the maternal body, literally forcing it to accommodate the growing child. By the twenty-fourth week the placenta, which is primarily a fetal structure, makes nearly all of the hormones for the pregnancy. A magnificently complex organ, the placenta metabolizes nutrition for itself and the fetus, protects the fetus from pathogens, prevents its rejection by the mother, functions as a "radiator" that monitors and controls fetal temperature, and, through several separate and distinct mechanisms, enables the transport of substances between the mother and the fetus (including oxygen and carbon dioxide, minerals, vitamins, and amino acids). My friend Michelle, a labor and obstetrics nurse, calls it pretty much the most interesting organ in the human body. "Aside from the brain," she said to me one afternoon at a barbecue, "there is not another organ that has such complex function. The heart, the lungs, the kidneys—all the other organs—pretty much have limited function. They do one thing. But the placenta, like the brain, is intricate and complicated. It is completely responsible for maintaining the pregnancy." Specifically, by producing the hormones that regulate pregnancy (primarily estrogen and progesterone but also human placental lactogen and human chorionic gonadotropin and pituitary-like and gonad-like and hypothalamus-like hormones) the placenta initiates all the systemic changes that make pregnancy physiologically possible. These hormones, primarily estrogen and progesterone, are largely responsible for the preternatural emotional qualities of pregnancy.

I began to understand that there are two kinds of life for women who bear children: Real Life and Pregnant Life. These correspond not so roughly to the real and the surreal. Ironically, the surreal life often felt more deeply real. Pregnancy was the thing that went bump in the night, the force that surprised me into my skin, the event that placed me in the here and now. Even as I anticipated a future radically different from anything I had previously known, pregnancy grounded me in the present tense. For me, this was a placid, welcome state. I became quiet and thoughtful, curled in on myself like a snail, ever reminded by the quickening that there were only two things my body needed to do, both of which unfurled unconsciously: Live, Nurture.

This pacific solitude also put me at odds with the rest of the world, and my dissociation from the so-called real world became clear one Friday night in March. The demands of our work, my fatigue, and our nesting impulses had conspired over the previous month to turn us into a shadow of the couple we had been. We had taken a hiatus from most of our dancing, and on weekends we stayed in, ate a good dinner, and, if we were feeling adventurous, rented a movie. Even quiet board games had fallen off our activity list. We hadn't seen our friends, nor even had a date out of the house. So it was with some anticipation that we decided to try a new restaurant. Most days I spent reading and writing, dressed (if you could call it that) in loose sweatpants, t-shirts, and Kory's old sweaters. Now, in our bedroom, I stood in front of our mirror and put on makeup, a black skirt, and a slim pink turtleneck that showed off my new bump. I put on heeled boots and loved how I looked. It felt like a first date.

Kory stood in front of the closet, in the nerdiest black gaming-convention t-shirt he owned, a ripped pair of jeans, and his hiking boots.

"You're going like that?" I nagged. "You can't go like that."
"Why not? What's the big deal?" he retorted.

"Because you look like a slob," I huffed. I knew that in San Francisco it didn't much matter, but it mattered to me, so he begrudgingly changed his jeans, switched his t-shirt for a v-neck sweater, and traded his boots for the Italian loafers he had bought on our honeymoon but which he hardly ever wore. Then he complained that his pants made his hips look too big.

I laughed. "No they don't," I said. But then I grew serious. "Can you try," I asked, my voice growing shrill, "not to look like a slob for just one night?"

An irrational fear took hold of me, and I was overcome by the thought of how he would look to our daughter, unshaven, uncombed, and padding barefoot around the house in stained t-shirts and threadbare pants. I imagined a slovenly husband in a slovenly home. I thought he would never again look like a respectable person who brushed his hair and wore clean clothes. What if fatherhood gave him license to dress like a homeless man? What if parenthood transformed us into the kind of people who wore elasticized waistbands and shapeless tunics and who didn't get regular haircuts? Of course, there was no rational reason for this premonition, and I knew, even in the moment, that I was possessed, altered as surely as Jekyll. But everything, large or small, anything at all was measured by my maternity. To his enormous credit, Kory understood this. He wore the pants.

The fight passed, and soon we were standing at a crowded bar, waiting for a table. It didn't matter that I couldn't drink the aperitif I wanted, that after forty-five minutes I was famished, or that after fifty my back was so sore that I hung, literally, on my husband. The restaurant was warm and pleasant. We were surrounded by stylish diners and lovely little plates of food.

By the time we were led to our table I was so distracted by hunger that I could concentrate on nothing but the menu and the crescent of bread between us. I devoured my dinner. In just a few bites I polished off two baby lamb chops grilled with herbes de provence and garnished with fragrant lavender sea salt. By myself I finished an indulgent, family-style platter stacked high with grilled asparagus tossed in Meyer lemon vinaigrette. Kory had Moroccan spiced duck with fennel and blood orange salad, but he picked at his food.

As I ate, Kory talked. He chattered about all manner of things. His work, the houses his colleagues were buying, the new season of reality television. I listened, glad he was in a social mood. But I contributed nothing to the conversation. With my head down, I shoveled forkfuls of food into my mouth. We must have appeared an odd couple, Kory with his hands in his lap, talking incessantly; me, head bent over my plate, eating furiously. I was certain it appeared we were fighting.

He told me about a new short film he had been working on in his spare time. It was, he confided, the most fully realized vision he had ever had. I knew he had been fishing around for a project like this, for something he could really dig into. He was convinced he had found the story, the point of view, the beginnings of the style; he was transported as he told me about it. He spoke swiftly and surely. His green eyes were bright, and he perched on the edge of his seat.

I could see all this, yet remained dispassionate. Selfishly, I couldn't bring myself to respond. I ate and he talked, and he talked and I ate, and as he talked, I ate his dinner, too. All around us the restaurant buzzed warmly, tabletops full of normal diners modestly enjoying the food and taking pleasure in each other's company. The only conversation I could engage in that night was about baby names. That was a conversation that was real. That was the conversation that connected me to my husband, not the one about all those artistic, creative aspirations we were supposed to be sharing. For baby names I was full of energy and ideas, but I felt empty, too, because I knew that there were other things that should interest me. Like art and books and film. Like my husband.

On the way to the car Kory turned to me. "I like spending time with you," he said. It was true. It had been a very pleasant evening, except for the fact that I wasn't really there.

The next morning we drove an hour to register at a baby "essentials" superstore. As Kory later pointed out, registering for a child is not at all like registering for a wedding, where you simply select all of the cool things you would like to own. After all, you know how you live as a couple, what you need, what you want. With a baby you become responsible for another life, and how do you know what you need for that? We needed onesies, but how many in each size? And sleepers, which apparently had to be chosen for the baby's weight as well as size. And bottles, so the sitter could feed her, but how many, and what brand? A baby bathtub, cloth diapers (again, how many?), mattress pad, crib sheets, changing table pad, changing table sheets, Vaseline, diaper cream, tiny baby comb and brush, nail clippers and file, medicine dropper. The list grew as we shopped. Who knew how many things she required? How was one supposed to know what she would really, truly need versus what was being foisted on our ignorance?

Even bolstered by a cell phone and the practical advice and supplementary lists of my mother and sister, we struggled through the store then spent an epic amount of time nervously pacing the stroller aisle. It is impossible to fathom the mysteries of the stroller until you have been initiated. Even then, no one is fully initiated until the baby has inhabited one for some weeks. Buying a stroller, the *right* stroller, is one of those classic catch-22 situations that all new parents inevitably face: you must choose the essential piece of equipment before you understand how it will be used. The stroller may, in fact, be the keenest foreshadowing of the learning curve all new parents face. Each stroller had one hidden, idiosyncratic mechanism for folding, another for reclining the seat, and yet another for raising the handle. Like cars, there were bargain models; compact, sporty models; handsome, streamlined mid-sized models; and trendy, elephantine models that could be compared to nothing short of an suv. That day, every other first-time mother and father we stumbled over as we paced the aisle was hypnotized by size: bigger was most definitely better. They wanted more padding, more storage, more presence. They wanted the gear that made manifest the outsized self-importance that consumed them, new parents to the end.

I knew that later, after the baby arrived, I would want less, not more. I would want to reduce the load I would have to push, carry, and haul everywhere I went. I knew that bigger was not better. No, bigger was definitely much, much worse. I longed for a stroller as slim and elegant as my pre-baby figure. That day, before the advent of sleek, modern, high-end strollers with insect-like names and futuristic designs, I surveyed a field full of contraptions equivalent to baby Hummers, unable to find a reasonable choice, and I despaired.

Kory and the other husbands appeared to feel differently. Strollers were gadgets to be conquered and things to be played with. They were manipulated long after the pregnant woman had decided that this one was too heavy, this one too light, this one could not take a car seat. No matter that none of the men could handle the mechanisms on their own, that a childless saleswoman half their age gracefully stepped in to demonstrate the mechanics and engineering. Display models littered the aisles as husbands jimmied and hoisted, pushed and pulled and tugged. They collapsed and opened the strollers repeatedly, as if trying to break a speed record. Of course, after thirty minutes of struggling with two models on our own, the area expert demonstrated which ones folded efficiently and which other inefficiencies were due simply to our own ignorance. We chose the sleekest model that we could find, one made in Italy, with a price tag that seemed to us somewhat indecent.

I learned many things at that store, including the fact that shopping for a baby was no fun. That it was, in fact, downright tedious. It seemed to throw both the responsibility of parenthood and our complete ignorance into high relief. I also learned that my husband really, really liked booties.

After, I cried.

I sat perched at a high table like humpty dumpty, waiting for a super vegetarian burrito. For the second time in twenty-four hours, Kory talked about reality TV. Tears rolled down my face. We were doomed. On the horizon I saw only dark clouds of trauma and misery. Startled, Kory turned to me.

"What's wrong?" he asked.

"Nothing," I said.

"Did I do something wrong?"

"No," I said. "It's nothing."

"Should I not be talking about this?"

"No. I'm just sad. Or tired." I sobbed louder.

"Are you sure I didn't do anything I wasn't supposed to do?"

I nodded, and then he walked over to my stool and held me. I was tired and hungry and overwhelmed, but none of these explained the deep sadness I felt. The sadness was a warm, dark bath of misery. I wanted to cry and cry and cry until the sadness streamed out of me, and I doubted very much that happiness would be hiding in the last tear.

Then it was over, and we ate lunch, and found in that unlikeliest mall, outside the multi-megaplex theater, nearly perfect ice cream. We sat in the sun on the concrete steps and gorged ourselves happy.

This is the rub: in pregnancy it is clear that your body is not your own. But neither is your mind.

While the rest of the world pursues its daily business, you are mired in the business of pregnancy. You forget how to have a normal conversation. When you do have one, it is sure to return to that newly supreme fact of your life. With my husband, I was all plans: the nursery, our finances, decorating the apartment, registering for the baby's things, even how we would make the most of our final three months together. I felt the rush of time at my heels. As far as I was concerned, between us was nothing but the baby.

Listening to Kory talk about his project that night at the restaurant, I was more than a little envious of his ability to care about something—*anything*—that was quite literally outside of himself. I worried that I would never have my mind back or my interests returned to me. I worried that after the baby, my myopia would only grow worse. Three months of pregnancy remained and afterward there would be long months of nursing. For months I had known that my life would never be the same, but I was finally beginning to understand some of the ways how.

This is the counterside to pregnancy's blissful moments of contemplation, a kind of coin flip of the psyche: the sustained inward glance is pregnancy's greatest blessing but also its most vindictive curse. Pregnancy distracts you from thought, from all the lives you know save the one that you own at the moment. The meaning of the haze may elude you, but its effect is one and the same: it distracts you from life—your life and all the rest of it, too—so that when you finally do become a mother, you may be all the more ready to give that life up.

THE LIVES AND
DEATHS OF MOTHERS

Spring arrived and, full of my not-so-secret life, I boarded a plane, my belly swollen like a small melon. I was six months pregnant and reluctant to leave my husband. Simply by being, the baby had formed another link between us, an umbilicus that subtly charged the connection we shared. Even more than when we had married, now we had the sense that we were in it together, hunkered down for the long haul, conjoined in a way that we hadn't been quite exactly before the baby. Kory was working long hours, but when he was home he was calm and full of energy. He took time to sit and talk every night, brought me decaffeinated coffee every morning. He still called me every day from work, and on weekends suggested things for us to do. We went out to eat, took walks, organized the baby things, shopped and cooked together. We danced several nights a week. Most everything was pleasant. It was almost as if we knew (though not consciously) that no one was going to do this but us, so we had better pay close attention to what we had.

Then, New Jersey was far away, and I was afraid that he or I would die. Partly this was due to the general paranoia, the palpable sense of mortality that infected the country in those days. Everyone spoke in grand and sentimental terms. Friends, family, even casual acquaintances and passing strangers in the supermarket embraced clichés about living-in-the-moment or appreciating-what-you-have or family-is-the-only-thing-that-matters. All of these things were no less true before September 11 than after, but many people—with and without children—seemed suddenly to have discovered them newly. My own fear was due as much to the simple fact of the pregnancy as it was to the facts of the world. Being so close to life reminded me constantly of death. It was not a morbid fear, and I didn't dwell on it, not exactly. Instead, I was innately, unconsciously aware that one did not exist without the other: that the opposite of life is death, that what I loved most—beginning with the baby—could be snuffed out, taken from me at any moment. Death was just as real as life, and the fact of one confirmed beyond doubt the immediacy of the other. Life and death thrust equally upon me, both equally real and equally arbitrary. Being so close to birth made me intimate with death.

Of course, there was something crazy-making in this state of mind. The hyperconsciousness could be deeply unsettling, and the experience of pregnancy was so new that it was, at times, profoundly lonely. I was used to being able to explain everything, to make myself known to others. But I was suddenly at a loss to communicate my experience. One of the things that makes pregnancy manageable is the tradition of it. You know that your mother, her mother, your husband's or partner's mother, her mother, their grandmothers had all done it. If you are lucky, the lineage extends laterally as well, through sisters and aunts, like a grid extending through time, enmeshing you in space, linking you all the way back to that first mother, Eve, or to the chimpanzee, however you would have it. All of them had done it, and I told myself that I would get through it because now I had no choice. Although it often seemed that no one had ever experienced pregnancy before me—that I was somehow different from all those other mothers—rationally I knew that this could not possibly be true. I let this thought tether me as often as I could, and I flew home to be with my mother.

My father retrieved me at the airport, and we drove through a maze of freeway interchanges, past the old Anheuser-Busch brewery with its iconic neon sign blinking *Eagle* . . . *A* . . . *Eagle* . . . *A* in the dusk. Newark tumbled upon us, block after block of brick buildings, broken sidewalks, rundown tenements. The city streets were familiar as the back of my hand. Life here was close and crowded. As we approached South Orange the hills rose in front of us, the city fell away, and maple trees draped their dark green embrace over the homes. It was as lush and fecund here as the city was hard and crabbed. My father confided in me, "I think your mother has been feeling guilty."

I looked at him as if he had told me my mother was pregnant. What could he possibly mean?

"She's been feeling kind of down. You know, the first child, the first pregnancy. She feels like she can't really be there for you."

Then I understood that I was not, in fact, coming home for a baby shower. I was coming home so my mother could see me pregnant. I was coming home so I could be my mother's daughter. I was coming home so that my mother could take care of her daughter, who was having a daughter, her granddaughter. While my mother already had two granddaughters, whom she doted on, this pregnancy was no less important and in some small but significant way different. When I was engaged to be married, my parents had taken Kory and me out to dinner, and there, in the restaurant, my mother had turned to Kory and said, "You have to understand, Kory, this is my first born, so if you make her unhappy, you have me to answer to." She said it with a smile on her face, and Kory laughed, but she was deadly serious. I understood not that she loved me more than my sister or my brother, not that at all. She loved me differently. It was a fact I would not understand for many months, not until long after my daughter was born. Then I would learn that the birth of the first child signals not just the beginning of her life but of your own life as a mother. Her nativity contains something of yours, and loving her will always be tangled up with that unlikely and startling transformation. My mother was to be witness for me. She would ground me and help me to understand what I could not possibly know, not for many long months.

At home I trekked through the wet grass and along the narrow passage that hugs the side of the house. The lawn was thick and overgrown from the early spring rains and the hedges were heavy with greenery. Mistaking the distance I had before me though I had walked that same path thousands of times, I brushed my belly awkwardly against the damp branches that draped across the path, painting my coat with dark strokes. My mother greeted me at the side door with a hug, "Hi, Mama," she said, and we both laughed.

We talked that night and for the next week about everything: the baby, the house, real estate prices, my job, Kory's job, their jobs, my old neighborhood, old friends and their new jobs, good school districts, child development, infant needs, my own infancy, my mother's pregnancies. We cooked and we ate, we shopped for baby and spent a long afternoon splurging on maternity clothes. I traded the sweatpants for a smart linen tunic, the sweatshirt for a short, snug jersey dress. We took long walks around the quiet neighborhood in the cool spring air. We napped. We continued talking. Knowing I would never again possess such selfish time, I rested and let myself be pregnant.

My mother and I had always been close, but that does not mean we had always gotten along. We are both prone to judgment and argument. We are both fiercely independent. I had an unconventional, rebellious streak that kept her awake many nights during my teenage and college years. We are both loathe to admit we are wrong, which can cause trouble not only in real, significant arguments but over stupid domestic things, like the proper recipe for roast chicken, or the facts of a current political scandal, or the particular merits of a new novel. But that week, things changed. Maybe she was finally ready to see me as an adult, my life in full throttle. Or maybe it was me, finally prepared to release my petty arguments and judgments. Or maybe I was so selfishly consumed by the pregnancy that it insulated me from other cares. Regardless—that week we were happy. My mother was happy taking care of me, and I was happy being her daughter.

In our family we had no tradition of mothering. There were just the three of us: my mother, my sister, myself. Both my grandmothers had died before I was born, and there were no aunts, no cousins, no other older women to whom we could turn, collectively, for advice. In fact, everything conspired against making my mother a good mother. She was a beloved only child, the only one of three pregnancies carried to term. My grandfather (or "Gramps," as my brother later christened him) married Catherine Donnelly in 1939, after tailoring his cobalt zoot suit to a more sober style in order to pass muster with her five older brothers. The first girl born to her parents but the seventh child in the family, my grandmother Catherine grew up in the suburbs of New Jersey, where my grandfather had recently begun working. Her father was a high-spirited, hard-drinking Irishman who had immigrated to the states during the latter part of the nineteenth century, in flight from poverty. The stories of his drinking are legion and apocalyptic. One involves perfumed rubbing alcohol, another vanilla extract.

At the time of their courtship, my grandfather lived in uptown

Manhattan with his sister, Ruth, in the neighborhood where he was born, which is now considered Spanish Harlem. He was a musician who played sweet—not hot—jazz on the mandolin with six other men. They called their band the Seven Strings of Rhythm. They had modest success playing at clubs and rent parties and even had a short-lived radio gig. After their marriage they moved to New Jersey and he more or less gave up the weekend binges, which continued without him for many decades.

Ruth married his best friend. Gene was handsome, with something of James Dean's rebellious, chiseled good looks. Gene taught himself to fly planes, invented a prototype remote control for his television, raised turkeys in the backyard of their Brooklyn home (and sold them at a profit), and jerry-rigged their home's wiring to tap into the electric utility pole outside of the house, in effect stealing power from the power company. Ruth was instructed to flip a certain switch when the meter man came calling so the meter would appear to be running normally. He built and installed a kind of swamp cooler in the attic of their home long before central air conditioning was available, and he showered Ruth with gifts. "He was a good lover," Aunt Ruth told me with perfect frankness over one of the long, intimate dinners she cooked for me late in her life. I was sure she meant this literally. "How's your lover?" she always asked me, referring to my then boyfriend, as if we were in perfect conspiracy about just how important this aspect of life was. After I graduated college and returned from my wanderings to live in New York, we had dinner together as often as I could manage the hour-long subway ride to her home in Flushing which, in retrospect, was not often enough. "He always came back," she told me once. This last fact was important because Gene often left the home to which he was so clearly devoted to spend his weekends in the city, where he played music and did other things that Ruth.

One Sunday night Gene came home with a baby, which most of the family later assumed he had fathered with another woman. "It's for you," he told Ruth, who had long wanted a baby. "We can't keep that baby!" she exclaimed. "Why are you bringing me a baby?" She promptly sent it back. Then Gene brought the girl home again, prompting the same argument, and back the baby went. This pattern continued, but eventually, after several months, they adopted her. As far as I know, no one ever discussed the truth of her paternity, but Marlene was the spitting image of her father and it would have been impossible to live with the two of them and not see the handsome resemblance between father and daughter. Whether out of respect or indifference or propriety, no one, especially not Ruth, mentioned this fact, nor even suggested it might be important. What mattered was mothering, and in this job Ruth thrived. After years of a childless home she had a daughter, and she left the job she loved with the telephone company to take care of her. My mother remembers her Aunt Ruth's home with the kind of longing usually associated with something that has never been. Imagine that 1950s ideal, with a truly happy woman at the center. That was, apparently, Ruth's home. Ruth cooked and cleaned and took care of Marlene, and always wore a neat dress. Even when she was nearly ninety her blazing white hair was perfectly done, and she wore full jewelry—diamond earrings, three diamond rings, a beautiful jewel-encrusted butterfly at her throat. She used her best china and crystal and had sweet little silver serving dishes that cradled pickles or squarish-round pillows of semisoft mints. It was neither precious nor formal, just comfortable and right. She loved her family unconditionally, she took care of them well, and they loved her back with equal devotion. I believe this impossibility because I knew Ruth. She was smart and funny and not without fault. She had a way of taking care of you that put you at ease. But the family's story does not end well. When Marlene was was nineteen and newly married she got sick and just a few months passed from the diagnosis of colon cancer to her death.

After my grandfather married Catherine they took the train straight to the World's Fair. They stayed in a boarding house and returned to New Jersey the following day. "We had to work," my grandfather shrugged. "We didn't have any money. Really, we were poor," he recounted once, as if the thought had just occurred to him. I badgered him about the fair. "Oh, well, it was amazing, really. The best thing I'd ever seen. We were happy, you know, just married and all."

At first they lived in a rented apartment on the top floor of an old house owned by a Polish couple. They, my grandfather and grandmother, were living there, in that apartment on Center Street, Piscataway, when my mother was born in April of 1940. They were still poor, but they were happy.

On weekends they shopped for records. My grandfather played the mandolin in the evenings and sang to them: "You are my sunshine, My only sunshine." Catherine taught my mother to double Dutch. They saved their money and bought a house with a yard. And then, not ten years after her daughter was born, Catherine was dead.

It happened suddenly and the facts are few. One Sunday morning my grandmother didn't feel well and stayed home from church. She might have had a headache. She lay down on the couch to rest. By evening she was dead. For years I was told (or perhaps I assumed) that she died of a heart attack. But she was only thirty, so this is unlikely.

I have never really thought of Catherine as my grandmother, only as the mother who was not there. The absent one. The one who was lost. I was twelve and constructing a family tree for social studies when I discovered the facts of her life and death. Because my grandfather had remarried, I had assumed that the cold woman I knew as my grandmother was, in fact, my grandmother. But even when she told me the truth, my mother was reluctant to reveal much of her past. Probably she was right to do so. At twelve I found the news unbearable and recounted it in horror to my best friend as we walked up the hill to school the next morning. My friend listened in appropriately stunned silence, piecing the story together, reconfiguring the family we both thought we knew so well. I was angry. I thought my mother had deceived me. But later I understood: what else could one say to a child? How do you tell your own daughter *my mother died* without conjuring up that terrific fear in her, too? How do you acknowledge that the motherless child and cruel stepmother of fairy tales—those twin horrors that you work so hard to dispel (*they're not real*, you say, *they're just stories*)—are, in fact, real and terrifying and decidedly *not* just stories. My mother's stepmother was cruel. She destroyed every picture of Catherine. She sent my mother away to live with her parents for the first year of her marriage to my grandfather. She threw away all of my mother's books and toys and her prized record collection. She made my mother clean the house and cook the family meals. It's no wonder my mother remembers Ruth's home so vividly or that she recalls it as safe haven, a place where mothers loved their daughters and took care of them. Even when I understood many years later that my step-grandmother suffered from severe postpartum depression and had lifelong battles with mental health, I could never quite forgive her.

The things I know about my real grandmother exist separately. They are fragments of stories, like dreams half-glimpsed or nightmares half-remembered. For my sister and me, Catherine acquired mythological status. The stories we heard were mostly of the good days, the plenitude of childhood, when everything is light and joy and love. There are darker stories as well, but, ostrich-like, we refuse to dwell on them. From my great-aunt Ruth: Catherine was the love of my grandfather's life. Every Saturday, if my mother had been good, they would go shopping and my mother was allowed to buy a record. One lucky weekend Gene Krupa came to town and the family went to the theater to hear the band. "He was amazing," my mother said.

There is a long list of things I don't know about Catherine's life and death. My grandmother doesn't have a coherent story, and, try as I might, I cannot make the anecdotes form one. She lived, she gave birth to my mother, she died. I do not know when or why she finally went to the hospital. I do not know how she died. I do not know who told my mother, or how she reacted to the news. I know nothing about the funeral. I have never been to her grave. I do not know what she liked to cook, what she found funny, how she liked to dress or fix her hair. I don't know if she liked to read or knit or garden, or what stories she would have told my mother had she lived. I know she had many brothers but I'd be hard-pressed to remember their names. Like her they died young, or were ripped from my mother's life by her stepmother and then died. I was twenty before I even saw a picture of her. I suspect that her image was shielded from us because, to this day, my mother bears an uncanny resemblance to her, to the one who died.

Over time I understood that for my mother, and so for me, motherhood was inextricably linked with motherlessness. I harbored always the fear and the knowledge of my own mother's death. I knew that it was only through the grace of God or a stroke of cosmic benevolence that we had been blessed with her presence. I ticked off my birthdays, her birthdays, measuring them against my mother's age, her mother's age, that fatal age. How lucky were we? How unlucky was she? This did not mean that our relationship was tranquil, but I never took it for granted.

After I returned to California I understood more. Something larger was at work. My maternity was not singular. It had a historical place, and I knew it could soften (though not redeem) the sad facts of my mother's story, even if it was also haunted by this same long shadow.

Then I wondered: What is it like to see your daughter transformed into a mother? Does it bring back memories of your own transformation? Do you remember the sea change that flooded your life all those years ago when she was born? Do you remember her birth, tending her infancy, watching her grow? Do you watch her and remember your own innocence, your own ignorance of life before her birth? Do you think of yourself, or of her? Do you think of your own mother? Do you see, newly configured, the impossibly complicated trinity of you three?

Perhaps my mother saw me moving toward life as swiftly as I felt its approach. Perhaps in that movement she saw one more chance to distance herself from death.

ROOM FOR
ONE'S OWN

As my due date approached, baby things threatened to overrun our flat. While it seemed my body could expand indefinitely to accommodate the child, our flat had no such capacity. Already she was greedy for space. The car seat and stroller rested against the wall in the narrow hallway. Beside these rested a baby sling, a front-carrier, a baby backpack. On one side of my desk loomed a tower of boxes filled with clothes from my sister. On the other I had sequestered the exersaucer, vaporizer, bathtub, and bassinet. Out of the bassinet rose bags of diapers, wipes, baby shampoo, diaper genie refills, baby books, and picture frames. Even the kitchen counters were beginning to accumulate large tins of formula, free "samples" that I kept even though I intended to breastfeed. For three months we lived with the clutter, which seemed to multiply parthenogenetically with the passing weeks. Three days after I taught my last class of the semester we began to reorder the apartment, reshaping our space in order to make room for the baby. I pursued this task with the single-minded mania that was my prerogative as a nesting pregnant woman. It was as if, by organizing the chaos of baby things, I could tame the uncertainty of my impending maternity. I was not exactly afraid of the baby, but I was wildly uncertain about what would happen to me after she was born. What—besides a baby—did it take to become a mother? What did one do when that day arrived?

More than the trappings for the baby, what disturbed my peace of mind most was what lurked in our own closets: the files, clothes, toys, memorabilia, art supplies and videos, old lamps, older computers, spare kitchen tools, a small basket collection, my vintage shoe collection, a broken hand vacuum, costume jewelry, old quilts, three afghans knitted by our grandmothers, spare picture frames, and a milk crate full of photographs. We had too much stuff and too many things that were irrelevant, or would quickly be made so in the months to come. For weeks I had been sorting through my office. When I left full-time teaching, a decade's worth of research and teaching materials migrated into our apartment. Organized by course, historical period, and genre, the stacks filled more than a dozen file boxes. Old essays, course readers, reference and research materials, even old quizzes lived in long rows of boxes, obscuring the floors of the closets.

Kory and I got to work. One weekend we stayed in our pajamas and starting at opposite ends of the apartment, began unpacking our closets and surveying our things. I moved swiftly, organizing, sorting, pacing from bed to closet and back again. Kory, on the other hand, sat down in the middle of the soon-to-be baby's room and slowly, deliberately, went through box after box, one paper, one artifact, one piece of memorabilia at a time.

After a week of sorting and discarding, two-thirds of my boxes still remained unexamined. We filled two carloads of donations and became expert at determining excess, distinguishing the valuable from the semi-valuable from the clearly useless and stupid. Of course this was easier to do with the other's belongings than with our own.

"What's this?" one of us would ask.

"A box," the other would answer.

"Do you really need it?"

Kory accused me of disrespecting his things. He was right, but so many things had never seen the light of day. The final sticking point was a stool: a three-legged, padded, brown, faux leather stool. It was one of three that had stood at the breakfast bar in his Glendale apartment and had lived a year behind the door in our dining area. It no longer had its mates. Yet Kory insisted it might come in handy someday. If he could find a place to store it, I said he could keep it.

"Where can I put it?" he asked.

"I don't know."

"Then I'll get rid of it."

This made me feel guilty. "Put it in the baby's closet."

"I thought there wasn't room."

"There isn't."

"Then I'll get rid of it."

"What would you use it for?"

"I don't know. It's handy. It's the same height as my butt." He sat on the stool to demonstrate. "You can use it to cook. When you make pasta."

"I stand to make pasta."

In the end I couldn't bear to force him to part with it. "Put it back behind the door," I said.

In fact, I had made one mistake and the stool was my attempt to make amends. In my nesting fury I had dumped a fat folder containing all of the material we had kept for teaching dance. It had contained a record of every dance class and workshop we had ever taught, every workshop we had ever attended, even the annotated choreography for some of our routines.

All too quietly Kory had said, "It would be nice to have a record of what we know."

In my defense, I did not think we would teach again. Nor did Kory, but that was hardly the point. I couldn't imagine a day when we wouldn't remember those routines (though that would come and I would regret everything anew), but the folder contained a record of what we had learned together. Not all of it, as Kory thought, but much of it. There were sequences of moves, styling tips, theories, a brief early history of the dance. It was obvious: I should have saved it, dance being one of the things that had brought us together. When I stopped to consider what I had discarded, I was filled with loss.

For years I had accumulated and hoarded things. Small knick-knacks and souvenirs from family vacations; birthday, graduation, and Easter cards from relatives; boxes filled with notebooks and journals; yearbooks; commemorative t-shirts; junior and senior high school projects; college essays and exams; gymnastics trophies and ribbons; and old books filled dozens of boxes in my own flat and my parents' attic. These represented my life, or parts of my life, and to discard them risked forgetting not only what I had done but who I once was.

As I sorted, I discovered that most of what I had accumulated I didn't need. It was neither valuable nor especially interesting. I hoarded to coax the past into the present. Now, change was inevitable and it was my responsibility to discern which parts of my past were as gravid as I was and which, lacking sufficient ballast, had become ephemeral. In those daily objects was an archive. It was up to me to discover the story.

Making room for the baby became a kind of archeological expedition. Confronting an old watch, Kory might announce, "This is from before I knew you," and decide to keep it, a souvenir of someone he had once been. Confronting an old necklace, I might declare, "This is from before I knew you," and decide to discard it, a souvenir of someone I had once been.

We worked swiftly but carefully as we chose what parts of ourselves to preserve and which artifacts might best remember us to our daughter. I kept my family things and anything written that had meaning: essays, bibliographies, nearly all letters and correspondence, but almost no cards. I kept school acceptances and offers of scholarship, college transcripts, select issues of the *New Yorker*, a stack of newspapers from the day the baby was conceived. I kept small keepsakes from my courtship with Kory: the scrap of paper on which he had written my phone number, the menu from our first Valentine's Day dinner, snapshots from a photo booth with both of us looking young and hopeful. I kept the tablecloth my father's mother embroidered, the gold and sapphire earrings I inherited from her. I kept dozens of my uncle's photographs, portraits of my family taken by him in the 1940s and 1950s that documented my family but also a way of life: my father careening down the street atop his bicycle, a ragged Pendleton flying behind him; my Pop-pop resting in his Adirondack chair on a dock at Shore Acres; my grandmother Lucy walking along the beach in her Sunday finery.

It might have been interesting to keep a list of what fell away from life in those days, a record of those moments and mementos that turned out, after all, not to mean much of anything. To make note of these things—like a faux pearl necklace from a young camper in Belfast, photos of me taken by a hateful ex-lover, a prototype papier-mâché pencil holder created by an artist friend, a vituperative letter written in the wake of a broken heart, floppy discs of juvenile stories, a bagful of foreign coins, political buttons from my days as an activist, a broken lighter from a broken-hearted Frenchman, preliminary dissertation research, rejections from literary magazines—those would have changed the story altogether.

Finally, the furniture was shifted, the curtains hung, the crescent moon–shaped lamp placed on the night table. The drawers were stocked with her first, impossibly tiny garments. The closets were emptied of all but those initial necessities: diapers, wipes, piles of pastel-colored receiving blankets, hooded baby towels, stacks of tiny washcloths, a small mountain of booties. Our daughter's space waited for her, cool and still as dawn. One day soon she would bustle in, and around her the room would assume its true shape, fitting first to her needs, then to her will. She would accumulate things, too: toys, shells, twigs, glittering rocks, dress-up clothes, art projects, blocks, dolls, books, hats, journals, CDs, scarves, fish and fish tank, scraps of paper, secret notes, lost teeth, feathers, jacks, pick-up sticks, stickers, so many things—all of them detritus, all of them indispensable tools in the trade of childhood. Like one of Joseph Cornell's boxes, her room would make perfectly surreal sense and make visible the collage of her. Like ours, her things would be aesthetic and useful or ugly and talismanic. They would define her to herself and broadcast to us something about her. We would have to make room for them and for her, over and over again. She would displace the space of our home in obvious and fatal ways.

This was why we both felt so ready to clean house. The baby on its way would reconstruct us. The space of our lives would have to accommodate hers. There was no room for the trivial, especially not for the solely nostalgic or sentimental. We had to make room for our daughter but also for the new selves we were becoming. Shedding so much of the past felt like cutting old anchors or tossing the sandbags out of the balloon so that we, too, could be borne aloft, anew.

LAST DAYS

The spring I was pregnant began bitterly, with a terrible, roaring wind. For two weeks straight the wind howled apocalyptically across the city and raged along our small stretch of coast. Angry whitecaps filled the shoreline and a whirlwind of sand made it impossible to approach the dunes. In southern California, gale force winds kept Kory's parents indoors for days on end, and we left our house only when we had to. The wind was biting and fierce, and despite my growing bulk, I felt as if the gusting would upend me. One afternoon we stood on the sidewalk outside our house and I jumped, over and over, letting the wind transport me backward down the street. Inside, we listened to the wind gust down the wide beachside avenues and heard its almost-human howling and the staccato clanking of flag poles. It seemed a sort of insidious companion. Its chill numbed me, inside and out, whether I was inside or out. I felt bothered and disheveled and found it impossible to think. Of course, it was easy to blame the weather, to substitute one tempest for another. It was not really the wind that had changed me, but it was an apt metaphor. That spring the wind was an appropriate incarnation of the change blowing through our home. We knew the end was rushing toward us, that we could not stop it, that we were in many ways completely out of control. Blaming the weather was convenient.

The one consolation of the wind was the clarity of the night. Every evening after sunset an inky black sky vaulted the Pacific. The stars were perfect points of light, constellations so clear it was easy to imagine them as maps for ancient travelers. There was Orion, journeying like a giant across the western sky, and Andromeda, and shining Venus. It was so beautiful that for a few breathless moments we'd brave the wind and step out onto the pavement in front of our house and stare skyward. The ritual was one thing, one shining moment to hold onto in the midst of the fury. This, too, might have been metaphor had I been able to remember that the baby was ballast as well as bora.

By early May I was still fearful and anxious but the breezes had calmed. The winds grew warm, and walking on the ocean path at midday about a month before my due date, next to the green sea, the waves breaking in an even rhythm, I was almost joyful. The ice plants, shaggy yellow and lilac flowers, bloomed along the dunes. On the path there were walkers, runners, bikers, mothers, and grandmothers with babies. I spied deliberately into each stroller, curious about what was inside, what waited for me.

I thought: there are years of motherhood ahead. Years of nursing and nurturing, rocking, tending, teaching. Once she was outside of me, the baby would take a long time to grow. When I stopped to consider it, the inside time, the long months that had so thoroughly tested me, body and mind—the months that had made me crazy and sick and crazy with happiness and sick with grief and anticipation—these were relatively brief. It would take the baby months to learn to sit up, a year to walk or talk, two more to be toilet trained. Five long years would pass before she would leave me for school. Now that I found myself at the end of the pregnancy, I knew it was just as certainly the beginning of something else. Many days I felt like spring, as if the baby had made me younger.

By mid-May I expected to go into labor any day. There was no rational reason for this belief other than the fact that I could look at the calendar and see ahead of me a short stretch of two weeks, then the due date, blocked off in black ink. Only four-teen days left, a solid block of time, two units easily absorbed by my eye. Change was coming very soon, and all I could do was anticipate. Inside me, the baby squirmed more. Every day she seemed to get stronger (or was it just my imagination?). She kicked less like a foreign object and more like a whole person. Her punch felt significant, as if she had weight, volume, and substance, as if the part that protruded from the left side of my belly might be attached to a whole body after all. Still, she was Frankenstein's monster to me. I could not wrap my mind around it—the baby, the labor, the baby after the labor, what was inside, what she would be outside, how what was inside would actually end up outside.

In late May, on a solitary afternoon walk, the contractions grew stronger and did not subside. They came sharp and cramped and peaked all at once. I stopped. They did not. I leaned over a fence post. I watched a fat black knuckle of a bee pollinate the yellow flower of an ice plant. I thought of our honeymoon: the cliffs of the Cinque Terre, the blue and rocky Mediterranean, the exact quality of morning light in Colle di Val d'Elsa. I breathed deliberately, exhaled through my mouth. The contractions stopped. I knew it was nothing compared to what was to come.

Two weeks before my due date, one Saturday morning, I had the first sign of the impending labor: my mucous plug fell out in the shower, followed by a straw-colored, then pink, then reddish brown discharge. It was mostly disgusting. The nurse at the birth center brought me in, not because, as I worried, my membranes had ruptured, but because I hadn't felt the baby move. They hooked me up to a fetal monitor to track the contractions and the baby's heartbeat. They did a painful pelvic and cervical examination and a biophysical profile. All were remarkable only for their normalcy. The baby was bigger, crowded, and positioned exactly where the midwife had said she was. She was head down and ready to go. *At least one of us*, I thought.

In spite of the hours of birth "class" and "preparation," in which I learned how to breath, how to use massage and ice and heat and the spa tub to ease the pain, in spite of our birth "plan," which outlined our preference for a "natural," drug-free birth; in spite of the fact that I would give birth in the Birth Center of one of the best research and teaching hospitals in the country, attended by a certified nurse midwife and a doctor committed to a safe, family-centered birthing experience; in spite of the fact that I would labor, give birth, and recover in the same room; in spite of the fact that I would have a private spa tub and private postpartum room; in spite of the fact that my daughter and husband would stay in my room with me (if I preferred); in spite of reading everything I could get my hands on about how it might proceed, I was still mightily unnerved by the prospect of labor. On the one hand, I was ready. On that one hand, all the dancing, all the yoga, all the studying had certainly prepared me for what was to come. But then, there was the other hand. And on that other hand there was nothing.

Of course, I was excited to see her, ready to get on with it, ready to be done with incubating. But there was no mistaking it: I was terrified. I had no idea what I was getting into. I wondered why I had gotten myself into this in the first place. My four-year-old niece exclaimed, "Ella is taking so long to get here." I was not so sure.

The last days were increasingly hard. I was swollen, heavier, nauseous. I felt disconnected, my body increasingly like a thing: a crazed, runaway, uncontrollable thing. It was not me, nor something I harbored. What was inside had taken possession of me. It had a mind of its own.

Most nights I was awakened by painful contractions, like a menstrual cramp, only exponentially more painful. My fingers tingled and grew numb. The insomnia returned. I could not sleep past four or five a.m. While Kory slept beside me, undisturbed, I lay awake in the dark, breathing deeply, thinking: *Not Yet.* One of these nights, or days, or midmornings, or late evenings the contractions would not stop. What was inside would push its way out, and our lives would never be the same.

In the early morning I lay in our newly configured bedroom, heard the birds wake and sing, listened to the hum of the ocean and the wind. I watched the sky brighten. I read by the first light of day. Longing for sleep, I enjoyed the unbroken peace, the quiet that would soon evaporate.

At eight or nine o'clock I would rise, shower slowly, endure more contractions. I checked email, invented errands. I bought stylish but practical shoes and my husband's first Father's Day present, a cozy, practical sweatshirt, deep green like his eyes. I baked biscotti and tried (unsuccessfully) to perfect my recipe for orange cake. I cleaned the refrigerator until it gleamed. Mostly I waited, attuned to everything that was—or was not—happening inside my body.

The end of the pregnancy brought forth nearly as much excitement and goodwill as its inception. Everyone I knew called to see how I was doing or, more accurately, to see if the baby had arrived yet. My in-laws, my local friends, my friends who lived across the country, our dancing friends, childhood friends, and parents of childhood friends: they sent emails from halfway around the world or letters from the far coast. My mother and sister called every day.

"This is killing me," Meredith said.

Her daughter, Elizabeth said, "I bet she can't wait to meet me."

My due date passed and I entered a no-man's-land of waiting, a new, more anxious expecting. I checked and rechecked the pregnancy books for signs of labor, as if I might be missing some vital sign. I stockpiled more food, spent endless hours on the phone with family and friends, walked miles along the beach. Still, she remained stubbornly, comfortably inside.

One week after my due date I arrived at my scheduled antenatal testing. They hooked me up to two monitors, one for the fetus and one for my uterus. They measured my fluid. We could see her clearly now. Her small face looked straight out at us, so real and human-like it startled me. Her features were distinct, newborn but unborn. She stuck out her tongue, swallowed, palmed the fluid. Once again the nurse thought she was cute. Her gestation nearly complete, she looked like a real baby. This was, and was not, comforting.

That night, Kory turned to me. "I want her here."

"Why?" I asked.

"So I can make funny faces at her."

I looked at him crossly.

"And talk to her and hold her, of course. Why do you think?"

I longed for nothing more than to be on the other side of pregnancy.

Day after day, finding himself distracted and unable to concentrate, Kory left work early. We ate, we walked, we watched movies or TV—anything to keep us occupied. Normal conversation was beyond us. Anything we said seemed superfluous. There was only the waiting. My mother said it was time to have a heart-to-heart with her.

"It's all right to come out," I told her on my morning walk. "The world really is a good place."

My husband lured her with sweet talk: "You can sleep and poop," he cajoled. But she took her time. I blamed her lateness on his genes.

In the end, at the end, there was nothing to do but wait. My brother-in-law is convinced that his youngest was the baby she was—petulant, demanding, irritable—because she was a scheduled c-section. She wasn't ready, he said. And they just yanked her out. There is no medical evidence for this, of course, but there is a kind of mythological, supremely superstitious quality to those last days of gestation.

The last week was the most difficult of the pregnancy—harder than the morning sickness, harder than the crippling sciatica, harder than accommodating my growing girth, much harder than preparing the house. In the final days I was a living list of prodomal labor: constant contractions, throbbing backache, bloody show, regular bouts of nausea. I had nothing to say to myself, my family, or my husband. I was a miserable, shrewish bore. There was nothing to do but wait. I was in limbo, caught between two lives, waiting for the *now*, suspended in *then*, a *corpus separatum*, a separated state, severed from everyone around me. My jurisdiction was entirely my own.

At one week past my due date I despaired. I had passed through every meaningful date. She had not come five days early (as all my mother's and sister's children had), nor one day before, nor on my due date, nor on my friend's due date (she having had the audacity to give birth to her son on my due date). Even sweeping my membranes—that uncomfortable, unnatural process in which my midwife digitally separated the membrane around the baby from the cervix—seemed not to have helped. My labor had not happened according to anyone's predictions, my mother's intuition, or nine months to the day after the baby's conception. There was nothing magical, mysterious, or superstitious about it; it was simply not happening. I felt as if I would never see her. I flirted with the idea that I would be pregnant forever, that my baby would never be born, that I would never find my way out.

INSIDE 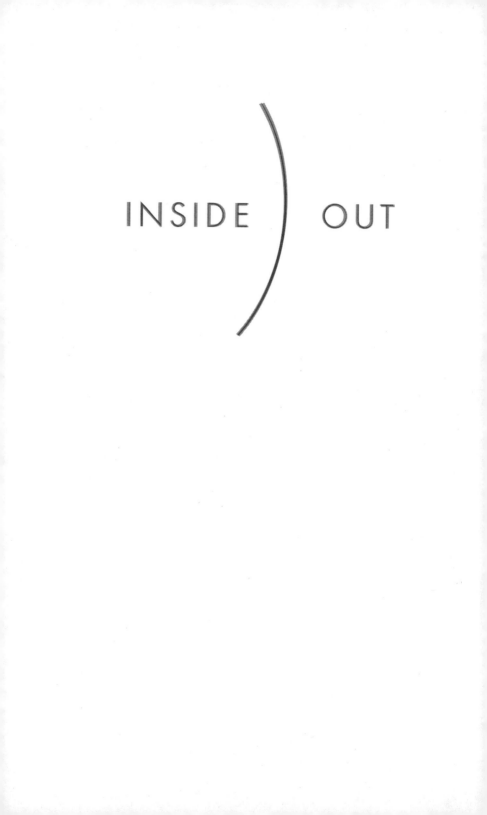 OUT

No one knows how labor begins. No one knows whether it is the baby who signals the body, *I'm ready!* or if the body tells the baby, *You're done!* or if it is some reciprocal agreement between the two, a pact made in the dark recess of the womb. Once it begins, it ambushes the body and takes the mother hostage. Its only constant is pain. It makes sense that clinical textbooks do not refer to birth as "delivery" but rather as "parturition," the process by which the uterus expels the fetus. Parturition is a better verb, invoking as it does all the violence and agony of birth.

First-time mothers and fathers know nothing. They fear labor will take them unaware, that its precipitous rush will deliver the baby suddenly into fumbling arms, that the birth, with all its blood and bodily fluids, will defile the living room, the taxi, the elevator in the hospital. They worry that they will miss the signs, that they will not know It has begun.

This nerviness is as unavoidable as it is unnecessary. First-time mothers are not singled out empathically for nothing. It was not until long after that I understood just how much knowledge informed that recurring question, spoken by strangers in the market, at the park, "Is this your first?" It was a question spoken from more experience, more knowledge than I could imagine at the time. My mother and sister repeatedly reassured me. "You'll know," they said. "You'll know."

Only in retrospect did I know my labor had begun. Late on the night of Tuesday, June 11, the contractions began and didn't stop. Every seven minutes one rose, pulling me from the edge of sleep. I curled my knees to my chest, rocked on all fours, shut my eyes tight. Ninety seconds of swelling pain, my belly drawn tight as a drum, then gradual, if incomplete, relief.

I dozed but could not sleep deeply. In the early dawn I stood in the shower, leaning against the cool tile, letting the water douse my swollen belly. The warmth blurred the contractions, rubbing smooth their sharp edges. At the center of pain I thought *It will only get worse.*

I stood in the shower until the water ran cold.

Morning arrived, gray and overcast. With nothing to do but wait, we dressed and walked along the beach, slowing down for the more difficult pains, walking through the manageable ones. The sand, sea, sky—all were of a hue, a sameness that made it difficult to determine dawn or dusk or even high noon. Where were we? Where was I? My body was our timekeeper, ticking out intervals between contractions. The hours, minutes, seconds—all the standard measurements of time—dissolved so that I understood time passing only as pain and then relief from pain.

I began to understand how women got though twelve-, twenty-, thirty-six hours of labor: inside labor time has no measure. There is only the getting through and, all the while, the knowledge of production. The pain of labor prepares you, primes you for the moment the baby emerges. For the first time in my life, pain had meaning, and that made the bearing-up easier.

One theory has it that labor begins when the fetus, sufficiently developed, releases a stress hormone that floods the placenta, elevating the production of estrogen and suppressing the production of progesterone. Estrogen promotes light contractions, the production of prostaglandins (hormones that stimulate muscle contractions and promote the formation of crucial gap junctions), and increases the receptors for oxytocin, the hormone that drives hard labor. While we know that the mother and the fetus—and likely the placenta—all play a major role in the initiation of labor, the specifics of the physiology remain unclear. In fact, the process is only slightly less mysterious than the astrological belief that the ensouled fetus, still so closely aligned with the other side, will coordinate the moment of its birth with the proper alignment of the stars that will chart its life's course.

Regardless, there are many old wives' tales about how to induce and speed up labor: true raspberry tea brewed from the leaves of the plant, a tincture of blue cohosh (especially taken in raspberry tea), castor oil consumed in varying doses and massaged into the belly may or may not be followed by an enema, a plateful of spicy food or regional specialties reputed to have mythical powers of induction. (A pizzeria in our area made a "Prego Pizza" loaded with thirteen toppings. Tales of its labor-inducing powers abound.) Any exercise that maintains the body upright and in motion—walking, cleaning, organizing closets—is said to encourage the process. In the first months of my pregnancy I was told to save some housekeeping project for my early labor, preferably a baby-oriented one like stocking newborn drawers with fresh packages of t-shirts, addressing birth announcements, or cooking meals to freeze. And there are more intimate and physical measures one can take, too. Nipple stimulation can release oxytocin, the hormone that causes uterine contractions, and there is always that old standby: sex, sex, and more sex. The prostaglandins present in semen can help ripen the cervix and begin the process of labor. Remedies like these are passed endlessly between women, their midwives, nurses, and doctors. The only surefire thing is that what works for one woman may not work for another.

Yet, as I was to find out, the much anticipated beginning of labor is only that: the beginning. Once in labor, you must tread that fine line between remaining active enough to allow the labor to progress versus keeping yourself fed, hydrated, and rested, because exhaustion will most certainly inhibit labor's progress. Labor is a natural process, but it is also really hard work.

Our walking did not, in fact, do anything except make me more tired, and back inside I sat splay-legged on a large blue exercise ball, bouncing gently as I talked to my mother, my sister, those friends who had only recently reached the far side of labor. The birthing ball, as we called it, took pressure off my hips and back and offered a strong mechanical aid to managing the contractions of early labor. I half listened as Kory tried to talk to me, to calm and entertain me. He bought sandwiches from the deli. I ate and rocked. I tried to rest. Early that afternoon we kept our scheduled ob appointment, where our doctor assured us we would have the baby by the weekend. It was small comfort. Back home I rocked through one, two, three movies. Late afternoon came and went. Between contractions, having nothing better to do, I advised a student on her thesis. I had not stopped working as my pregnancy advanced, and my summer work consisted of advising several students on their projects. The work gave me a flexible schedule, which I thought I could easily do in the weeks up to and just following the birth. My student and I spoke on the phone for a long time about her book as my contractions came in gentle waves. As my silence in the wake of her question grew unnaturally long, she would ask, "Was that a contraction?"

"Yes," I answered, "but it wasn't too bad."

We ate a light dinner. Evening came and went. Bedtime approached, night fell, the twenty-four-hour mark passed, and it became clear that I would not sleep for a second night. Near midnight, racked with pain and fatigue, I called the hospital. As I already knew, the delivery did not seem imminent.

"You can probably stay home a while longer," the intake nurse advised.

"Okay," I said. In spite of the time that had passed, I knew I was more comfortable at home. "I'll see how I feel in a few hours."

"Call us back if anything changes," she assured me.

I lay back down to a steady assault of contractions. Two hours later I was back on the phone.

"I'd like to know what's going on," I said.

The nurse's voice was sure and empathic, a voice that understood the hours I had passed. "You just come in and we'll check you out. We'll see what we can do to get you some rest."

A good OB or labor nurse or midwife can tell if you are ready to come to the hospital simply by the sound of your voice on the phone, by the way your voice catches or stops when a contraction takes over. Their job is to keep you talking until the contraction comes, to listen to what you don't say, what you can't say, what you are forced to say through the pain. In my case she heard not the coming delivery but the long fatigue. She sensed that I had reached the limits of laboring at home. She sensed that I needed help.

I took a short shower, Kory loaded the car, and we drove through the quiet summer darkness to the Birth Center. I felt as if we were the only people alive, and although we were driving on familiar, well-traveled streets, we seemed to be driving through the underworld. It was a dark passage, not to hell, of course (though the pain would later take on that quality), but a passage to a fearsomely unknown place. Also, by then another worry had begun to plague me. Though I had played down this fact with the nurse, I suspected that my water had broken.

There are many myths about childbirth. To start, first labors do not generally begin with a bang, with one unmistakable contraction. One does not rush headlong to the hospital. It may take up to ten hours to progress from the onset of early labor to the more precipitous and vastly more painful contractions of active and transitional labor. In my case it took much longer. First labors almost always take time. While the average labor for a first-time mother is fourteen hours, for a second-time mother it is only eight.

Second, although labor is a natural process, this does not mean that it comes naturally. Like the anxious parents who wait for the baby, the body is similarly unschooled. The uterus is spastic and doesn't really know what to do. The baby moves slowly, and the descent into the birth canal is measured slow centimeter by slow centimeter. Then, the pushing is not the volcanic expulsion we imagine; for the first-time mother it can last an hour or more. Finally, and perhaps most surprisingly to anyone whose notions of childbirth derive from film or television, the rupture of the amniotic sac is not always sudden, nor is it unmistakable. This most dramatic signal of labor occurs only in about 10 percent of women. For most, the waters will break after labor has begun, usually in the second, or active, stage. For others, like me, the sac may rupture early, with the onset of labor, but its slow leak can be difficult to detect. Conventional medical practice has it that once this rupture has occurred, the baby should be delivered within twenty-four hours. To wait longer risks infection for both mother and child.

I knew all of these things but that knowledge did not help

my body labor. I was strong. I thought I was mentally prepared. But my body might as well have belonged to a different woman. Hour stretched into hour and nothing significant occurred. Just as there is a term for a woman in her first pregnancy, *primagravida*, there is also a term for a woman who delivers a child for the first time: *primipara*, from the Latin *primus*, first, and *parere*, to bring forth. The body must learn the process of labor. Mine, apparently, was a very slow learner.

In the Birth Center, hooked up to fetal and uterine monitors and the automatic blood pressure gauge, I sat on the high table in a long cotton gown, legs akimbo, sipping cold cranberry juice. The room was very white, the ward empty and quiet. I was the only patient, a fact that heightened the surreal atmosphere of the place. We waited and listened as the baby's heartbeat rose and fell with a rapid tom-tom beat. I watched the numbers on the monitor steadily blinking with my baby's heart rate and waited for the mountainous spike of the uterine monitor that came with each contraction. The normal fetal heartbeat ranges from 120 to 160 beats per minute, and we watched as our baby's heart stayed solidly within this range. Out of the monitor spooled a long strip of paper mapping the duration and intensity of each contraction and the drop of the baby's heart rate during each assault. We watched the white snake of paper cascade rhythmically to the floor. After some minutes we waited, watching the uterine monitor for another spike, but the line stayed flat. The monitor confirmed what I already knew: my contractions had stopped.

Prolonged labor and failure to progress are not uncommon, especially in first births. When my mother was pregnant with my sister, she experienced a similar arrest upon arriving at the hospital. The attending doctor, a cantankerous old man, chastised her: "You got me out of bed for this! You don't belong here. Go home!" The nurses kindly took her aside and assured her, "He needs to retire. Stay here and rest." Six hours later she delivered my sister. The experience was traumatic enough that three years later, upon discovering she was pregnant with my brother, she stood at the kitchen sink and cried. I was assured by my nurses that women's labor often stopped in the Birth Center. Some, they exclaimed, stopped laboring in the parking lot. In fact, all mammals will cease to labor when they feel threatened, afraid, or uncomfortable. It only makes sense that we have an evolutionary instinct not to give birth if we are surrounded by predators or uncertain about the environment into which our babies will be born. No matter how kind and how reassuring my attendants were in that moment, I was still exhausted and anxious. I felt I had failed.

As the doctor prepared the speculum, Kory asked, "Is there a bathroom?" And then, with a sort of convulsion, he fell.

"Hold him!" the nurse cried, reaching across my enormous belly. "Hold him!" she repeated, as I wavered. Hold him? Wasn't I the one having a baby? Then Kory slumped against me, and I caught him. I could smell the wool of his sweater, the sweat in his hair. He was heavy, and I struggled to keep him from falling. I thought he was having a seizure. I thought something was wrong with his heart. I thought *How could he do this while I was in labor?* I thought, with a blind flash of fear, that he was dying. Out loud I called his name; inwardly I called God. In an instant the tiny room crowded with another doctor and two more nurses. One intrepid nurse tore smelling salts from the back of her ID card and broke them under his nose. With a shudder, he came back.

In the chatter of voices we learned that apparently husbands faint. Mine would be fine. "Just make sure there's a chair behind him for the delivery," the nurse with the smelling salts warned. What had appeared to me a seizure was his body catching itself as it gave way to gravity. He had simply fainted standing up. The nurses quickly discerned that Kory had neither eaten nor slept much in twenty-four hours. They found him juice and some crackers, then led him to a cot in the next room. He ate slowly. For the next thirty minutes, as I discussed my condition with the doctor, he lay quiet and ashen on a couch at the far end of the room. To this day he swears it wasn't the speculum.

Although my contractions had all but stopped, the pH of the fluid marking the strip of Nitrazine paper and a speculum exam confirmed the waters pooling behind my cervix. My bag of waters had ruptured. I knew immediately that this had probably occurred a day earlier. Since the amniotic sac protects the fetus, sealing it off from the outside world, when a woman's water breaks the womb becomes like an open wound, creating real danger to the baby and mother. While amniotic fluid replaces itself every three hours, without IV antibiotics the risk of infection is great. Infant mortality increases significantly when premature rupture of the membrane occurs more than twenty-four hours before the onset of labor. In fact, in the nineteenth century, puerperal fever, the infection that killed Mary Shelley's mother, was epidemic, spreading from patient to patient or from autopsy to birthing room, usually by doctors' unwashed hands. While the epidemic, exogenous form of the disease is now rare and treatable with antibiotics, puerperal infection, which now most commonly occurs as endometritis (an inflammation of the uterine lining), may be caused by bacteria naturally occurring in the genital tract or elsewhere in the body. While at least one clinical textbook terms such infection "common" and suggests that it may often be mild enough not to require treatment, the infected postpartum patient must be carefully monitored and isolated from others on the maternity ward because the risk and consequences of infection remain serious. After my daughter's birth was over and after developing a fever in spite of the antibiotics, I realized that without modern medical care I would easily have died in childbirth. My daughter, too, would have been dead.

There was more bad news. In spite of twenty-four hours of contractions, I had not yet entered active labor. My cervix was dilated two, maybe three centimeters. While there is great variation in individual labors, and enormous variation in what is considered a safe and normal pattern of progression, parturition consists of three stages: labor, pushing and delivery, and delivery of the placenta. Labor, the first and most dreaded stage, consists of three phases: early, active, and transitional, during which the cervix is said to "ripen" like a piece of fruit, if much less appetizing.

Throughout the pregnancy the cervix is rigid, increasing in mass, water content, and blood flow. Like the uterus, its plasticity changes so that, according to one textbook, "it combines the properties of a rubber band with those of salt water taffy." A combination of connective tissue, primarily collagen and smooth muscle, the cervix must soften and distend in order for the fetus to be expelled. This process, controlled by a complicated mix of hormones and enzymes, often begins well before the first contraction. As the collagen is enzymatically degraded, the cervix softens and effaces. Normally an uneffaced cervix is shaped like a donut, about two centimeters thick. As effacement proceeds, the cervix will retract and be pulled upward toward the uterus, finally becoming paper thin, at which point the dilation, or opening, of the cervix begins. It is this measurement that provides the measure of labor's progress, because until the cervix has dilated from zero (fully closed) to ten centimeters (fully open), it is impossible to birth a baby vaginally. Dilation is also the measure that provides the first real shock of labor's physiology. When seen actual size, the diagram of a fully dilated cervix has the circumference of a large orange, an object that appears impossible for your body to accommodate. Before delivery, though, it is easy to forget (or ignore, or suppress the fact) that something much larger than this will be passing through you. After delivery, this fact no longer matters. Relative to the baby, effacement and dilation function much like pulling a sweater over one's head. It is not so much that the baby is pushed down and out of the uterus as that the cervix and uterus begin to be pulled up, over the head of the baby.

The three phases of labor correlate with the dilation of the cervix. During the first or early stage, through the pressure of regular contractions the cervix dilates to three or four centimeters in diameter. In active labor the pain of the contractions increases dramatically as the cervix dilates to seven centimeters. While this phase of labor tends to last about half as long as early labor—on average four hours—the contractions last longer and become more frequent, and their pain is more intense. The final phase of labor, transition, sees the cervix dilate fully, from seven to ten centimeters. This is the phase when contractions come fast and thick, and they reach maximum intensity almost immediately. It is a time of absurd pain. Women cramp and shake and vomit. They curse their husbands. They say: I can't do this! They want to give up.

I had many centimeters to go, and because of the early membrane rupture I needed antibiotics and, to my great dismay, Pitocin, a synthetic version of oxytocin, which is used to augment or induce labor. Both of these required an intravenous drip. I resisted. The resident doctor sat at the end of my bed.

"Let's talk about this. What's the word on the street about Pitocin?"

"That the contractions come faster and harder and are more difficult to manage. That it usually leads to an epidural." I explained that I wanted to be active during my labor. I wanted to be able to walk, kneel, bathe, squat—positions widely regarded as more conducive to labor and delivery and which are vastly more beneficial in managing pain.

Midwives have long known that laboring upright helps labor progress. Movement helps a pregnant woman manage her pain by enabling her to find the most comfortable position at any given moment; it can also help the baby descend into the birth canal and align itself properly for delivery. This descent exerts even more pressure on the cervix and further hastens dilation. Standing, sitting, squatting, kneeling, even side-lying positions are to be preferred over the more conventional lithotomy position, where the mother lies on her back, her knees bent and lifted above her hips, her legs splayed wide and held in position through the use of stirrups. Lithotomy is a position historically used for surgery on the lower abdomen and reproductive organs and provides no physiological advantages for the laboring woman. In fact, lithotomy can interfere with and complicate delivery. Consider the benefits of working with gravity rather than against it as you labor to deliver a seven- or eight-pound object out of your body: staying upright is simply common sense. In most non-Western societies, upright positions for labor and delivery are considered normal, and squatting during delivery seems to be the most beneficial position of all since it promotes fetal descent, enhances the engagement of the head with the pelvis, and widens the pelvis by as much as 28 percent.

Fortunately, I gave birth at a major research hospital where doctors had, according to my obstetrician, learned "everything they knew" from their midwives, who had been part of their practice for two decades. So, even with the augmentation of Pitocin, the resident explained, I could be given a labor experience as close to my wishes as possible. She could begin with a very low dose of the synthetic hormone and see how I responded. She could give me morphine to help me sleep.

I cannot remember the first stick of the iv, or the drip of the Pitocin, or the antibiotics, but I do remember the morphine. The drug washed over me quickly. I felt my heart rate rise, my head grow heavy, and a great dimness descend as if a scrim had been dropped. My vision became opaque. I was afraid.

"My heart is racing," I said.

"It's probably the morphine," the nurse assured me. I felt drowned. I understood obliquely the lure of heroin. It was hot and frightening and then, suddenly, it was not. I welcomed the oblivion. After thirty hours of labor, I slept.

Early the next morning I woke in the labor room, a spacious corner suite atop the fifteenth floor of the hospital. Later, neither my husband nor I would be able to recall how we had arrived there. From every point of that room, with its two long banks of windows, I commanded a view of San Francisco. To the east the Bay Bridge surged from the city to Treasure Island to fog-banked Berkeley. Westward the city's hills swelled, topped with green banks of trees and pastel blocks of apartment buildings. Beyond them stretched the vast gray expanse of the Pacific, and the majesty, even at such distance, of the Golden Gate Bridge. Over the next fifteen hours it was a view I would scarcely glimpse, but it was there on my periphery, an open space where my mind wandered blankly between contractions. Kory lay across the room, curled on the sofa, covered by a thin hospital blanket. I lay in the white bed, on my back. I called to him. He woke slowly. We took in the gray morning rising around us. For a moment we seemed to float there, suspended above the city, safe. And then I was inside the pain.

The Pitocin had done its job. While sleeping I had entered active labor and dilated another two centimeters. This time, I was grateful for the pain.

All day, I labored. I labored standing beside my bed, one arm on the IV. I labored horizontally, bent over a table, gazing blindly at those excessive views. I labored as I slowly paced the room, sometimes supported by Kory, sometimes as far from him as I could get. I labored on all fours, then collapsed onto my forearms. I spread my legs to accommodate my belly and labored there, bent over in child's pose. I labored in bed, seated like a tailor, rocking gently forward, as the pain expanded inside me. I labored lying down on my side when the exhaustion became too much. I labored on the large blue exercise ball in a deep, leg-spreading squat.

It used to be that women were taught complicated breathing patterns to help them labor and push the baby out. The Lamaze techniques were designed by Fernand Lamaze, a French obstetrician, in the early 1950s, and throughout the 1960s Lamaze revolutionized childbirth education. The techniques aim to help women labor "naturally," without drugs or anesthesia. Like the Bradley method, another natural method, Lamaze encourages the father or partner to be actively involved in the labor. But natural childbirth education really began in the 1930s when Dr. Grantly Dick-Read, an English obstetrician, suggested that women's labor pain is compounded by fear and ignorance. Through education, relaxation techniques, and breathing exercises, he argued, such pain could be minimized. Though not directly influenced by the early pioneers in pain research, together these first proponents of natural childbirth understood that labor pain—like all pain—was partly subjective and could be modulated by experience. That was the radical thing: the pain of labor could be controlled by the laboring mother, not by the medical establishment.

The result has been something of a revolution in labor pain management. Now, any progressive, mother-centered, midwife-informed labor education class will tend not to tell you to ask immediately for an epidural or teach you how to breathe in patterns—a virtually impossible task for a woman in the throes of labor. Instead they will offer a range of techniques for pain management, only one of which is medication (and the epidural is only one of these). Labor pain is productive pain, our instructor said over and over. It is not unremitting. You will have pain, then you will have a moment to recover.

There are many ways to manage labor pain without drugs, and the more of them you know the better prepared you can be for your labor. Changing positions and vocalization—also known as moving and screaming—are among the most essential. Heat therapy, cold therapy, water therapy (including the use of a shower or whirlpool), massage, guided imagery, aromatherapy, meditation—all are used by laboring women with varying degrees of success. Such techniques are directly related to Melzack and Wall's gate control theory of pain, since anything that helps the brain modulate the gates that transmit pain to the brain can affect the mother's experience of pain. In other words, nonmedical techniques of relieving labor pain, often associated with midwives and folk remedies, work because they stimulate the gates that control the sensation of pain in the first place. Most women who have benefited from these practices will proclaim loudly the inestimable value of the midwife, the doula, the labor and delivery nurse. Because it's a fact: no matter how much your husband loves you, no matter how supportive he is, no matter how fierce and unflinching his devotion to your labor, your husband is fundamentally ignorant. It might make you feel a lot better to have him in the room, or his presence may be irrelevant to you, or he may infuriate you (as my brother-in-law did to my sister during her first labor by ordering a pizza delivery to the birthing room; later, to his enormous credit, he was indispensible in saving her life when serious complications emerged). But a good midwife or labor nurse can make the difference between a drugged labor and "natural" one. She will encourage you to walk, to breathe, to focus (on the pain or away from it). She can massage and manipulate. A friend confided that her midwife was so skilled in her art that when she laid her hands over my friend's belly or massaged her back in a specific way, the pain of the contraction evaporated. These skilled women can talk you through each contraction, its beginning, its swollen, mind-splitting climax, its slow release. Their talk helps take your mind off the pain and reminds you, too, that although the pain is immediate, vertiginous, and critical, it is not lasting. You get to the end of the voice and you find the end of the pain. You follow the narrative the midwife tells you, the arc of the pain, the story of each contraction—for each contraction is an epic descent into one more circle of hell with an eventual, miraculous climbing out— and you know it will end.

By early afternoon my pain had escalated. I sat on the blue ball, rocking and circling my pelvis, trying to find a way out. The narcotic fentanyl, which I had been taking for two hours in 100-gram doses, no longer took the edge off the pain. Now the contractions came fast and hard, and the relief between them was minimal. In the middle of that pain, at pain's deep center, it was dark. In that dark there were no others and there was no language. It was silent and it was deafening, it was still and it was cyclonic. My body shook with the effort, or with the pain, which by that point were one and the same thing. I was sure my body would rend itself in two, forgetting for a moment that that was exactly what it was doing.

As the uterus becomes increasingly coordinated, contractions peak simultaneously in all directions. This demonic coordination is made possible by the formation of gap junctions—bridges or pores that facilitate the passage of signals between cells. Gap junctions allow messages to pass nearly instantaneously throughout the uterus so that contractions occur without mediation by the brain. Although they are absent or infrequent in the normal uterus and decrease dramatically within twenty-four hours of labor, during labor approximately one thousand of these junctures exist in each cell. Gap junctions are what allow for the involuntariness of labor, for the sense that one has of being overcome, for the symphonic, harmonious explosion of pain.

On the edge of tears, certainly on the edge of exhaustion, I climbed into a warm bath. The jets were turned on and I let the water massage the contractions. Kory sat by my side. He may have held my hand. He may have counted. He may have talked to me. For some minutes the waters were lethean. I felt soothed and almost human. Then the heat of the water seemed to rise and the contractions intensified. I thought I would drown so I hauled my enormous dripping self out of the waters.

When my midwife checked me I still had not progressed. Then I gave up. Bearing up was one thing, being worn down was quite another. In short order the anesthesiologist administered an intrathecal dose, a temporary spinal block that eased my pain immediately, and then an epidural. I was fitted with a catheter, then an internal fetal monitor. I lay on my bed, and waited as the pain subsided. Finally, I slept the sleep of the dead, or the damned.

At eight o'clock they checked me again. Still no progress. "We'll give you one more hour," the doctor said. "Do you know what this means?"

"Yes," I nodded.

"You know that we don't do these for just any reason. We take these very seriously. But after one more hour I think we will have tried everything." His manner was sedate, even kind, but it was also matter-of-fact. At this hospital they did, in fact, try to avoid Cesarean sections, and that they had waited so patiently for my labor to resolve itself by itself was, by now, ample proof of their commitment to me and my so-called birth plan. If my doctor thought it was time, it was time.

"That's fine," I said. And it was fine. I had one overriding impulse: Get her out. Resigned to a c-section, I lapsed into fitful sleep.

An hour later the resident woke me, checked me, and consulted with the doctor. "You're going to deliver this baby vaginally," he said. "Are you ready to push?"

I hardly understood how, after so many hours of stasis, progress was possible.

"I guess so," I said quietly.

Later I learned that extreme fatigue, such as I had experienced, can actually inhibit labor's progress. This, or extreme pain, or anxiety can release catecholamines, which inhibit the ability of the uterus to contract. In such instances sleep may be necessary, and it might even be clinically prescribed in the form of sedation, since sleep can suppress the release of the catecholamines. In my case it may have been that my baby's head finally turned in the proper direction relative to my pelvis, or that she finally exerted the necessary amount of pressure to complete my dilation. Or maybe I simply needed to rest.

Then came the pure relief, the strength, and the victory of pushing. After the epidural it did not hurt much, and for this I was profoundly grateful. I had had enough pain, enough strength and grit, enough bearing up. I sat up in the hospital bed as best I could, my legs splayed and supported on both sides by two nurses, and I pushed down, and down, and down, concentrating all of my physical knowledge on contracting the muscles I could not feel. The resident coached me: "Do not blow out, this diverts your strength." "Push out in one long breath." I pushed down through my womb, not out through my lungs. I directed all my breath, and used all of my training to focus my energy down, and out, and down, and out. Years of working with my body began to pay off. She moved, a fraction of a centimeter at a time. The nurses and my doctor all but cheered. The baby's head appeared and receded. Appeared and receded again. This is another thing they do not tell you: in labor the ground you gain can also be lost. Especially, as in my case, if the baby has not fully descended by the time the cervix is fully dilated. My friend Michelle, when attending births, would often let a fully dilated woman labor until she felt that urgent need to push. She would guard the door to the room and lie to the doctor: "No, she's not ready yet." When the woman was truly ready, she would summon the doctor. "Why push too early?" she says. "Why spend all that energy when nature will do it for you if you just give it time?" But time was not a luxury that I had that night, so I soldiered on, pushing through the increasingly great contractions. In spite of the epidural, I tired. I rested. I pushed again. And then her head appeared, crowning between my legs. I reached down to touch the roundness of her scalp, her damp hair. I saw a black, matted mass. It frightened me. It almost repulsed me. An alien, it seemed, was about to emerge. I do not know if I was squeamish about her, or frightened by the threshold I was about to cross. I had yet to push her out. It hardly seemed possible that I would not be torn asunder, that the pain would not be unendurable. Perhaps this was the real reason my body had been so reluctant to deliver her up. It knew my fear better than I.

Looking back, I realize that although my labor was much longer, and more comprehensive than most (meaning I experienced many of the technologies and aids available to modern laboring women), it was not more difficult than most, nor even necessarily more painful. There are many more serious complications, many more intervening and unkind doctors, many more emergency interventions that can be done. Labor is a natural process but this does not mean that it unfolds easily. My labor was belabored but it was not unusual.

For me, even in the end things did not go smoothly. The baby's heart rate fell. My temperature rose.

The doctor was patient but firm: "She's fine now, but she may not be in twenty minutes." I trusted him. There was something in his manner, unhurried but vigilant, that reassured me. "He knows," my resident had said earlier. "He's delivered thousands of babies." Drugged and dazed as I was, I knew this. I knew it simply by his look, his touch, his gentle but confident authority.

He remained calm, jovial even, as they brought in the vacuum, which did not work. The pump was broken, and for the first time in forty-nine hours I became truly frightened for the baby. I waited. They fiddled with the rickety looking machine. They fiddled, I waited. Finally it was in place, and I pushed as the resident, guided by the doctor, helped ease Ella out. I heard the doctor guiding her calmly through the procedure. I listened, somehow outside of myself, even in those crucial moments, aware of the details, the expertise, the care they took with my body. One long push, a pause, a continued push, a straining that pained me intensely even through the drugs, and then, there was her head, enormous and black with hair rising between my legs. "Oh my God!" I exclaimed, and then, with one easy push, her body slipped out and it was over.

Because of the vacuum extraction, I could not immediately hold her. They whisked her away to a warming table and I watched a circle of white-clad backs, bunched tightly around her like a coven. I heard her squall, listened to the flat recitation of her Apgar score.

Kory walked over. "She's fine," he said.

"Go back to her," I commanded. I strained to catch a glimpse of her, then delivered easily the placenta, a robust, crimson mass the size of a dinner plate. I had thought it would repulse me but I felt only two things: relief that the final bit of birth had been expelled, and that predictable pride that my body had created something so healthy and sustaining. I waited and waited, strangely patient, for my first full look at my girl.

After many minutes of attention, after hearing her thin, pitchy cries, after the cleaning, the testing, the weighing and the diapering, after the afterbirth emerged, heavy and dark, Kory walked her to me, swaddled and new. He held her to my side and I gazed at her. I called to her softly, "Hi Ella, hello love." Recognizing my voice, its pitch, its tone, something she had heard so many times before in her dark womb, she turned to me. She turned to me and I took her from her father. She was my child, so much mine and so unknown to me.

More than a year later a friend remarked that having your first child is the transformative event of your life. On that table, she said, you too are reborn. Today I think that what mothers gain through their birth stories, what makes mothers different from other women, is not so much knowledge as experience. Childbirth is experience as knowledge, experience that is impossible to divorce from knowledge. Much as we like to metaphorize it, childbirth is not metaphor. As agonizing as any creative act might be—such as birthing this book—it does not hurt. It does not literally turn your being inside out as you give up part of yourself to the world. All at once, that which was inside you is suddenly out, and you lose and gain in a bloody moment of life. That loss of heat, the seven or so pounds of baby that was inside of you, that simultaneous loss and acquisition of life, so startling and wet, often causes the body to shudder and shake uncontrollably, as mine did. Afterward, I lay on the birthing bed and shook and shook, like a Shaker moved by her God. Birth is a moment beyond belief, a moment after a moment of pure being, the beginning of a love that is knowledge incarnate.

Of all my achievements, none is so wondrous to me as my daughter. But it is no wonder that, even as mothers, we look around the world and see simply other people. If we saw what we truly are, remembered the void and pain from which each of us emerged, the truth would, as Emily Dickinson knew, dazzle us blind.

) OUTSIDE

THE FOURTH
TRIMESTER

In the pictures taken immediately following the delivery, I hold
Ella, a tiny bundle with transparent, waterlogged skin, her eyes
alert and questioning, as if she is startled by the world. I, on the
other hand, look horrible. My skin is blotched and sallow. My
hair sticks up in clumps. My eyes are haunted, dark half-moons
void of light. A drugged smile lists across my face. But in those
first moments I felt only relief and hope.

Ella emerged a taut, squirming, desirous thing. Even the
nurses were surprised by the ferocity of her hunger and her innate skill. I did nothing but hold her to my breast, and she began
to suck. In the days that followed she seemed not a baby but a
small, feral animal, so insistent and grasping was her hunger.

When she was sated and awake, she was all eyes and ears.
Every new light or shadow occasioned a pause, the newness
registering across her face as difference without, of course, comprehension. We witnessed almost immediately her prelingual
knowledge that in this bright, new world there existed things
beyond her body.

Dismissed from the hospital and sent on our way, I walked down the hall on shaky legs, past the postpartum rooms, past the labor and delivery rooms, past the intake rooms, to the single bank of elevators. We had walked those same halls just two days before, but now they were strange and unfamiliar. I would not have been surprised had the walls fallen away or the floor crumbled beneath me. Kory seemed to be an actor, playing the part of the new parent, carrying his daughter down the hall. I suppose he was. I was, too. With Ella capped, swaddled, and blanketed—but placid and alert—we descended the elevator to the rest of the world. It felt very much like we were getting away with something criminal—stealing a car or finding a bag of money that definitely did not belong to us.

Driving out of the darkness of the underground parking structure and into the bright morning, we were acutely aware of our cargo. She looked so tiny and fragile, tucked snugly into her car seat, like an egg cradled in the cup of its shell. How could we have been entrusted with such a thing? What were we to do now? Kory drove slowly down streets it seemed we had never seen before. The car seemed enormous. How could I never have noticed what a dangerous machine the automobile was? There were hazards everywhere: other cars, stop signs, lights, pedestrians. Even on a sleepy Sunday there seemed to be so many *things* in the world.

Kory drove with both hands planted on the wheel at ten and two o'clock. He crept to a stop at each intersection, looked left and right, then left, then right, then left again. He waited until neither man, woman, beast, child, car, truck, motorcycle, bus, streetcar, bicycle—not any living or moving thing—was within range of the intersection, then he proceeded slowly to the next stop sign. The world seemed large and dangerous. Above all, it seemed utterly new. When we finally arrived home and stopped the car in the driveway, only then was I able to breathe freely.

It was reasonable that I felt different, worse in some ways, better in others. More surprising was the apparent transformation of the world that I thought I knew so well. It was as if, during my labor, those pains had wracked the very fabric of time-space, warped it, so that now my universe had a new center and a new circumference. Things no longer occupied the same relations as they had before Ella. Now that she was here, everything posed a problem or an opportunity, a new experience of pleasure or of pain. I saw the world differently, and it wasn't simply because of how I could and could not manage the stroller, though there was that, too. Everything took on a new relation, in relation to Ella, everything now had meaning for her as well as for me. Our home was her home. Did she need light or should the shades be pulled? Music or quiet? Would the noise from upstairs wake her? How would the ocean appear to her? Or the gulls squawking over the backyard, or the massive, coal-black ravens who sat in the middle of our wide street?

I thought I still knew who I was (*I am in my car, with my husband beside me*) but I was not at all sure about the world to which I had been transported (my baby was beside me, too, and what kind of world had made *that* possible?). Much later I came to understand that *I* was the uncanny thing, the thing out of place, that thing that I knew and didn't know. I had changed right along with the relations of my world, but it would be many months before I would understand the contours of my new self.

By the time we arrived home I was exhausted but I followed Kory and Ella up the stairs and into our flat. It felt cool and empty and much larger than it really was. It did not seem the right place for a baby. We stood in the entryway and looked at each other, then around the apartment. We stared blankly. Where should we put her? On the couch? The floor? The bed? The bassinet? Her room or ours? It seemed a monumental decision, what to do with her. It seemed there must be a right choice but we would certainly make the wrong one. She was totally out of place, and so were we. We set the carseat in the middle of our queen-sized bed but it looked awfully precarious and lonely sitting there by itself. Able to think of nothing else, I unstrapped the harness, lifted her out of her carseat, and decided to keep her with me, which was where she belonged anyway. Kory unfolded the sofa bed, changed Ella's diaper, and then placed her, swaddled, on the bed next to me. I tucked a thin blanket around me so I could be covered without smothering the baby. Ella lay close to my body, my arm circled above her head, and she felt like a warm, solid little thing. I lay still and let myself get used to her. Soon Kory joined us, and we rested, all three of us, in the afternoon sun. It might have been a few minutes, it might have been an hour. The flat was quiet. Ella slept. We lay there being a family, for a long time out of time, wondering what would happen next.

It took me a week to recover from labor. I slept every moment I could. Wrapped in pajamas and a blanket I lay on the pull-out sofa in the living room. Ella was beside me all day, a tiny thing beside my huge, sweating, aching body. I woke and rolled over to nurse her. Otherwise, I was so thoroughly spent that I rose only to shower, sat up only to eat, left the house only to visit the doctor. Even these short outings exhausted me. I slept, Ella slept. Kory slept, too, but I was not sure when. Most nights, he and Ella were awake through the early morning hours, watching World Cup soccer.

After the pain, after the bone-soaking fatigue, came the hunger. No one had prepared me for this. No one had warned me just how hungry I would become in the days after I gave birth. Even as the fluid left my body through urine and sweat—a horrible, cold sweat that soaked the bedclothes and necessitated two or three showers and two or three changes of pajamas each night—the milking left me ravenous, as if my stomach had been emptied along with my breast of every scrap of food and nutrient it might have possessed in reserve. I could never eat enough. Every few hours my blood sugar dropped precipitously, and it was all I could do to load myself with calories. I ate handfuls of nuts, chocolate, dried fruit, crackers, cheese, olives, meats, antipasto vegetables, cold pasta, cold pizza, salads gifted by friends. I was grateful to the point of speechlessness for the food my friends had dropped off, because even the ready-to-eat meals I had stored in our freezer took too much energy to prepare. Truly, it took Herculean effort to defrost and reheat and serve. Then, on day three of Ella's life at home, an enormous, cement-heavy box arrived via FedEx from New York. I sliced it open and revealed a half dozen cheeses, olives, artichokes, flatbread, a loaf of dark rye, dolmas, roasted peppers, black olive tapenade, marinated mushrooms all slick with green olive oil and pungent with vinegar, and a large box of buttery, orange shortbread. Ravenous, I gazed at the bounty and wept. It was exactly what I needed. I could hardly believe my friend's goodness. We ate our fill, and then, like the loaves and the fishes, the food sustained us for many days.

The first six weeks postpartum, often referred to as the fourth trimester, is a deceptively arduous time. During this period the mother's body must reverse all of the processes of pregnancy. Every system of her body, not simply her reproductive organs—from respiratory to gastrointestinal to hematologic to neuromuscular—has undergone dramatic physiological change in order to assume the additional functions and capacities of pregnancy. After birth, the mother's blood volume, which has grown 30 to 50 percent, by up to a liter and a half, must decrease to pre-pregnancy levels. Her heart rate, which has increased progressively over the pregnancy until it beats fifteen to twenty times more per minute, will slow. The concentration of thyroid hormones, which have been elevated in order to support the altered metabolism of carbohydrates, proteins, and lipids, must return to normal. Placental hormones, like estrogen and progesterone, diminish rapidly. The mother's uterus must shrink and resume its proper relation to the rest of her abdominal organs. The cervix, bruised and distended from delivery, must heal, or "form up" and shorten. The site of placental attachment also must heal (which it does, amazingly, without scarring). And, of course, breasts, under the influence of two powerful hormones, prolactin and oxytocin, must undergo the final transitions that will enable lactation. This is only the best-case scenario: there are many complications—from surgery to depression to placental retention—that can make recovery much more arduous.

And then there is the practical matter of the baby.

With the first one you simply do not know what to do. Thirty-six years earlier, my mother had been handed a baby. She looked down at me and experienced no flood of joy. What now? she wondered. By her own account, she was terrified. They had no car seat and no cradle, and I slept nestled in the sturdy white box in which they had transported me home from the hospital. That box rested on the car's rear seat, then later on my parents' dresser. On her first day alone, which was my second day home, my mother laid me in the center of the bed and stared. She had no mother to turn to, had taken no child-rearing classes. No one had shown her how to diaper or nurse. Beside her bed was Dr. Spock's thick volume. It would stay there for a dozen years, until all three of us had passed safely through our childhoods, until she knew the skills of motherhood like she knew her own breath. But first, on that first day, she sat on the bed and thought *What now?*

A baby is not a regular person in miniature, but a bundle of indecipherable needs. Ella was mysterious, possessed of her own logic (if one could call it that) and her own internal rhythms of crying, eating, evacuating, and responding to the world, which alternately interested and exhausted her. A baby's first little movements are unpurposeful, experimental only in the most radically unconscious sense of the word. Like all other babies, she was literally a network of reflexes: rooting, sucking, grasping. Lying unswaddled on her back, her legs pumped up and down in the walking reflex; when startled, she arched her neck, threw back her head, extended her arms, and then all her limbs would rush together in a weak convulsion known as the Moro reflex, by which she looked as if she were about to beat her chest or rail her fists against us. She might turn her head to one side or the other or extend the opposite arm like a fencer in an odd exercise known as the tonic neck reflex.

At nearly eight pounds, Ella was not an especially small baby, but as she lay next to me those first days she seemed tiny. Even the preemie-sized jumpsuit bagged around her belly and ankles. Underneath her thin, transparent skin, her blood vessels were visible in little tetrahedron patterns, spidery webs of red veins. Her five-year-old cousin likened her skin to salami.

When I looked at her in those early days I had trouble understanding where she had come from. First she was inside me and then she was outside me. There seemed little correlation between the birthing and the baby that had emerged as its result. Surely, I had seen her head push into the world. Certainly, I had cried out in surprise and shock as I saw her head crown, large and black and wet, and felt myself stretch to my farthest limits—but no farther—and then the rest of her appeared. Yet, after, she was a miracle too large even for the ordeal of her birth. Its trauma in no way equaled this reward. She was mine, and yet she wasn't.

So we lay there learning each other, skin-to-skin, as close and naked as possible. Two days after we arrived home, my milk came in. I watched in awe as milk dripped from one breast like water from a very leaky faucet, while Ella drank from the other. Ella gulped, her eyes widening as if she didn't quite know what to do with all that bounty. Then she slept and squawled and sucked on my breast some more, which had grown to ridiculous proportions (just how enormous I didn't realize until I saw, in a picture, my breast as large as her head). I lay beside her as often as I could, in part because I was exhausted but also because my rest was prescribed by the labor nurse, the midwife, the pediatrician. Mothers are often encouraged to spend time in close contact with their new babies. Such contact facilitates the bonding between mother and child, offers warmth and comfort for the baby and, most important, stimulates the pituitary gland to produce oxytocin, the hormone responsible for ejecting milk from the glands to the ducts to the reservoir in the areola. This "let down" is the crucial process that allows the baby to nurse; until it begins, the baby is without a significant source of nourishment (the colostrum and transitional milk that precede it are rich in fluids and immune-boosting antibodies but not in fat or nutrients).

Oxytocin, also known as the love hormone, has myriad and complex functions in the female body. While it drives labor and nursing, it is also released during orgasm and its production during nursing accomplishes two things. In the early weeks it causes the uterus to contract, sometimes with painful cramps that help the uterus shrink back to its normal size. From weighing approximately 1000 grams at delivery, the uterus rapidly shrinks to about sixty or eighty grams by six weeks postpartum. Oxytocin is also responsible for the rush of sentiment, the calming sensation that new mothers experience and which may be heightened during nursing. Many times over the coming months I would collapse onto a chair or a couch, harried and frustrated and stopped in my tracks once again by the needs of my fussing, hungry baby, and then, as she sucked and the milk began to flow, the let down coursed through my breasts with pleasant, tingling warmth. I would breathe deeply and be suffused by a peace that was purely physical, completely beyond language and emotion. She would eat and I would rest, and there was nothing more to be done. Other times, at the end of the day, when I felt like a droopy dog, the same action would nearly put me to sleep. Nursing, I often found that I had no choice but to relax, to empty my mind, to gaze at my baby, or to lose myself in a book or a hypnagogic reverie. Thus sentimentally manipulated—my own complex, psychological love addended by the biological wash of hormones—I, like most mothers, fell deeply, irreversibly in love with my child.

Like pregnancy, labor, and birth, nursing is a natural, biological process that must more or less be learned. Usually both mother and baby have work to do before it becomes the effortless call and response, the overly sentimentalized but still very real symbiotic relationship between nourishing mother and satisfied baby. Perhaps no postpartum activity is as closely or anxiously monitored as breastfeeding. And perhaps no postpartum activity strikes so near the root of a woman's sense of self-worth as a mother. But nursing is as biologically complicated as it is emotionally fraught.

For a baby to nurse properly at least two things must happen. First, she must latch on properly. Second, she must suck correctly. A baby does not actually nurse from the nipple, but instead forms a seal with her mouth on the breast, her gums over the entire areola. To accomplish this seal you might first brush the baby's cheek with your finger, or tickle her chin, or prime her mouth with your nipple. Then, when she is finally wide-mouthed, fully agape, in that very instant you must thrust your breast into her mouth or her mouth onto your breast. It is neither delicate nor graceful nor especially attractive. At first it is desperate and uncertain. Move too slowly and she latches on to just a part of you, causing you great pain and her great frustration. Sometimes the feat of latching on can take many minutes. After that the baby must learn to control the flow of milk, to create the negative suction that will secure the breast in the mouth; she must learn to play her tongue (which is enormous in proportion to her mouth) against her palate, in a rhythmic, undulating motion from nipple to areola. She must learn to coordinate expressing with sucking with breathing with swallowing. An infant's cheeks are many, many times stronger than an adult's. In fact, they are among the strongest muscles in her body. They contain sucking pads that help to stabilize the mouth during nursing. But still, even with these adaptations nursing does not always come easily for the infant. Difficulty latching on, an inefficient suck, difficulty controlling the flow of milk—all of these things can cause frustration for mother or infant or both. There is also, always, the problem of learning not just how to feed, but when. The mother must figure out when the baby is hungry and must learn to decipher hunger cries from wet diaper cries from gas cries from tired cries from just plain-and-simple cranky cries. She must learn to decipher the cryptic and random facial expressions that can also signal hunger. For instance, all newborn babies purse their lips and pulse their mouths in an odd fish-like gesture called rooting, which is a sign of hunger. In fact, if you are very observant, or very lucky, you might be able to discern this fact before your baby begins to cry.

Mastering this timing can be a difficult thing for new mothers. Babies' faces move often and unpredictably, their eyes dart, their mouths open and close, their muscles twitch. They are expressive but not in the same way an adult or even an older child can be. Like most new mothers, I was exhausted and uncertain about pretty much everything except the fact that I was exhausted and uncertain. It would take many weeks, months even, before Ella's expressions would signify anything meaningful for me. I suspected she was hungry? cold? fatigued? gassy? I pretended I knew what she wanted, but for the most part I felt very, very dumb.

It used to be that women were helped in these skills—knowing when and how to feed—by mothers, sisters, aunts. As age and geographical movement for education and jobs have dissolved this intimate, local support system, many women now go it alone. Some turn to friends, a community breastfeeding support group (a chapter of La Leche League, for example), a lactation consultant from the hospital, or a good, well-trained postpartum nurse. In fact, a whole industry has arisen to address the many different ways that nursing can go wrong and to help women find ways to make it more convenient and comfortable. There are breastfeeding aids and accessories and advisors and experts. There are chat boards and blogs and forums and leagues. There are special clothes and bras, slings and nightgowns, privacy shields and supportive pillows. There are endless, incessant, stealthy, tearful, prideful conversations.

Even though Ella was undeniably excellent at nursing, and larger than 95 percent of the babies her age, and gaining weight steadily, still it was not easy. I availed myself of a reasonable number of supports, but most of the time I was alone with my baby and I found it very easy to be unsure how to manage it, this simplest and most complicated of tasks. I twice got mastitis—a common but extremely painful breast infection that is accompanied by fever and incredible soreness and which is cured with the aid of antibiotics and nursing quite brutally on the infected breast. I worried constantly that I was feeding Ella too much or too little. Which is to say, I found the psychological aspect of breastfeeding to be easily as challenging as its physical task. Even after I had been nursing for what were a relatively trouble-free eight or ten weeks, a nurse consultant remarked, "Oh that's not very long at all." For me, it had seemed a lifetime.

In those first weeks it was as if my body had been taken away from me, then given back. I felt stilled, more quietly attuned to the sensory world. After the first, arduous recovery, I felt preternaturally calm, utterly content with the goodness of life around me. The intense passions that I had sought most of my young life seemed shallow in comparison to the deep tides of

contentment that pulled at me now. My daughter's smile trans-
ported me to a bliss beyond that of any adoring lover's gaze.
Sleep, to sleep, an unbroken hour or two or three was sheer joy.
Mornings were always Christmas.

Awake, I watched Ella's tight fists wave in the air, her oblong
orb of a head turn toward her father's voice, toward my breast,
toward the arc of light falling from her moon lamp. Her newborn cry was high and thin, a voice from another planet, almost
that of another species. She was a little warm machine, eating,
burping, spitting up, falling asleep, sleeping, waking. Hungry,
her mouth pursed with those little fish breaths. Deep in the bassinet she slept, capped, swaddled, and tucked between blanket
rolls, a little breathing, mouthing, vomiting thing. Kory would
reach out to calm her, his arm hanging over the edge of the
bed, searching the bassinet for her compact, swaddled form.
He slept often with one hand on her chest. Then, at eleven
p.m., one a.m., three-thirty a.m., six-thirty a.m., he would rise
and hand her to me, the stiff, swaddled bundle of her filling my
arms, my arms encircling her whole being. She smelled sweet,
like my milk.

After Kory had returned to work, I woke twice a night for
the feedings. Until this time he had risen, changed her, and
brought her to me. Once I was more fully recovered, I would
slip out of bed at her first cry so as not to wake Kory for longer
than necessary, though in truth he often didn't hear her cries at
all. Mostly the night feedings were painful stumblings through
crushing fatigue. Sometimes they were something more.

A short dark hallway connected our room to Ella's, and to
walk that cold night passage was a journey from something familiar to something new and strange. In her room I switched
on her moon lamp, a yellow gingham crescent that, when il-
luminated, glowed with a pale, unearthly light. My head spun
with sleep as I plucked her from the crib, lay her swiftly on the
changing table, fighting the mounting anxiety provoked by her

hungry cries. I changed her blindly, and by the time I was finished she was frantic and grasping with hunger. I picked her up, and her head lunged for my breast. She missed and latched onto my bare arm, her toothless gums surprisingly sharp against my flesh. I moved swiftly to the couch, offering my breast with as much speed as I could muster, but in her eagerness to nurse she latched onto my breast just above my nipple, sucking so hard a bruise would bloom in the morning. She was all need, all desire, and I could barely keep up with her insistent, aggressive hunger. And yet, finally, she and I would settle ourselves, and then she could drink steadily. I looked down at her, exhausted but unwilling to close my eyes. Here was peace for both of us, a still center in the middle of the exhausted, dark night. I couldn't forget what came before and what would come after, but I let myself sit in that moment. A bliss possessed her, so pure and so uncomplicated that I was certain its pleasure would never be surpassed. A friend of mine would later demur, arguing that more complex pleasures were best. To my eyes, my daughter's joy was complete, a perfect moment of desire fulfilled. And in that moment with her, if I didn't experience quite the same perfection of longing satisfied, I was given a glimpse of that paradise we had lost, and that primal memory was enough.

After those first moments of suspended animation, we learned something else about parenting a baby: infants eat time. I began to think of Ella as some manner of black hole into which our hours vanished. While it appeared on the surface she did nothing but eat and sleep—all infants spend sixteen to eighteen hours per day in sleep—it took unreasonable stretches of time to complete the deceptively simple tasks she demanded. I held her and comforted her, her tiny uncontrolled body surrendered to me and to the impulses of her immature nervous system. I wiped the gunk out of her new, puddly eyes, caught the spoonfuls of spit-up that poured out of her mouth after each nursing, changed the sleepers that were soiled several times a day from the same spit-up. I changed diapers, a task at which I fumbled for many weeks. I rocked her and sang to her when she fussed. I bounced her when she fussed especially hard. I checked the baby book each time her poop changed color, or when I forgot how to clean the dark, shriveled stump of her umbilical cord. I worried about whether a pacifier might cause nipple confusion, or what could possibly be causing the spit-up. I nursed her to sleep and then held her quietly, for many minutes afraid moving would wake her. I lowered her gently, oh so slowly, into the bassinet. Swaddled and nestled between blanket rolls, she slept, her little fist balled in an arrested wave, her thin lips pulsing involuntarily with the memory of nursing, the only thing she truly knew. There was no end to the cycle: feed, burp, change, swaddle, sleep, feed, burp, change, swaddle, sleep, bathe, dress, feed, burp, swaddle, sleep, change, dress, feed, feed, feed. In the interim there were showers for me to take, meals to prepare and eat, a house to clean, laundry to drop off, and always, always sleep to catch. In those first hours and weeks time closed in around me. I lived from nap to nap, craving that deep, blissful rest that would restore me, even if only temporarily, for the next round.

So quickly did Ella become part of the fabric of our lives that we forgot there had been a pattern, a life before her. When she was just three weeks old Kory turned to me: "I can't remember when you were pregnant," he said. I thought a minute, then admitted to him that neither could I. We stared at each other in wonder, and laughed a little at our idiocy and at how different life now seemed to us. We both *knew* I had been pregnant, but what our lives had been like before seemed so obscure, so distant from our current domestic arrangement that it was beyond us to imagine we had even *had* a life before Ella. Our collective amnesia was partly due to exhaustion and our limited mental capacity, and partly due to the immediacy Ella demanded of us.

With all the feedings and changings and walkings and regular housework and other "real" work and our own eating and (trying to) sleep, there was simply no time to think about what had been before her. The amnesia was also due to the fact that she had transformed us. We fell head over heels into the immediacy of her and were happy to let her rewrite our lives. Not much of what came before Ella really mattered anymore, except inasmuch as it had prepared us for what we were doing now. There's the old cliché: life doesn't end when you have kids. But for us it did end, totally and completely, and then it began again.

When Ella was three weeks old, I left the house by myself for the first time. She had woken us early, and it was a bright, warm Saturday morning, the kind of clarion day that made me remember why I loved California. Kory stayed home with Ella and as I drove along the Great Highway, the Pacific stretched a deep, placid blue all the way to the horizon. I made my way across town to the farmers market I attended as religiously as church. As I crossed the quiet, cobblestoned side streets, the world seemed remade. Around me the morning was still, nearly Edenic. My body no longer pained me, and full of milk I felt ample and productive. Liberated from my home and my baby, it seemed very much as if I had been absent from the world for a long time, and it had changed.

I approached the market warily, dogged by the feeling—but really it was a knowledge—that I had forgotten something. I felt slight guilt over the luxury of the hour I had stolen from her, but I was more exhilarated than not. No one but me knew that there was one more baby in the world, and the secret of her life buoyed me. I thought the world was being revealed to me in its true form, for the first time, and it really did seem bright green and full of promise.

At the market the stands were piled high with summer's elaborate harvest. Just looking made me happy. It was so early that many of the stands were nearly untouched, and I had my pick of produce: Arctic Snow peaches, tiny seascape strawberries, hot and sweet Pimientos di Padrone, black Bing cherries, Flavorking pluots, and bushels and bushels of tomatoes—pink & yellow Brandywine, Green Zebra, Early Girl, Elephant Heart, Pineapple. As my bags filled, they hauled me back to my past self, to life before Ella. On the way to the car, famished, I plucked a ripe Early Girl from the top of my bag. It fit perfectly in my cupped palm. I took a bite and savored its smooth, taut skin, its thin, sweet juice, and for a single moment I remembered I was more than her mother.

That afternoon Ella cried and cried, unable to soothe herself to sleep. I lay her on the bed next to me and took down a large volume of poetry. I read her "The Lotos-Eater," and let my voice inhabit Tennyson's murmuring, melodious assonance.

> There is sweet music here that softer falls
> Than petals from blown roses on the grass,
> Or night-dews on still waters between walls
> Of shadowy granite, in a gleaming pass;
> Music that gentlier on the spirit lies,
> Than tired eyelids upon tired eyes;

Never before had I been so truly, so deeply inside the mariners' fatigue or their longing for sleep. Never before had I been so like the mariners in the midst of an epic journey, so tired of laboring, so willing to be seduced out of the world. Magically, Ella quieted. Her eyelids drooped. Miraculously (it seemed), she slept.

I buried my face in her neck, nestled my cheek against her downy hair, inhaled the lotos-like perfume of her sweet milky smell. I wanted never to let her go, never for her to grow, never to journey away from the shore of her or this deep moment of dreamful ease. But, of course, I did not want to embalm her, nor could I let myself be seduced by the opiate of her forever. I tried to imagine living in what Gertrude Stein calls the eternal present, that impossible idea of experiencing time out of time: a moment after a moment after a moment, my daughter's life, my life in my daughter. If anything could alter time, could alter the most fundamental way I experienced my life in this world, I knew then that it would be my daughter. It would be the difficult labor of becoming her mother.

HATCHING

Like all new parents, Kory and I were exhausted and it wasn't the kind of fatigue from which one recovers. There was no way to sleep in, or catch up on all of the sleep we had lost in the night, or take any break at all from Ella's demands to be fed, changed, rocked, soothed, walked, and fed again. She was always there, and she almost always needed something. "I'm still tired from Elizabeth," my sister said to me one day on the phone while my head buzzed and hummed with sleeplessness and it seemed to take effort even to breathe, "and she's five." Even though I learned very quickly to nap when Ella napped, and I often slept as frequently as Ella did, for months I slept no more than four hours at a time.

Babies are born awake, and for the first few hours they experience a period of quiet, alert wakefulness. It is a suspended moment, a brief interregnum before the gravity of the world asserts itself. Then they sleep. Over the next twenty-four hours they establish a pattern of sleeping and waking but, unlike adult's sleep, a baby's sleep pattern is not tied to hormone levels, nor to night/day patterns, nor to body temperature rhythms. While the newborn baby possesses high levels of melatonin, one of the major hormones regulating sleep cycles that passes to the infant through the placenta from the mother's bloodstream, once this melatonin has disappeared it will take months before the baby can manufacture it independently. So until body temperature and hormone production are regulated (at around three months of age), an infant's sleep patterns are by nature and function different from an adult's. A baby might sleep during the day and spend the long night hours awake. (This is how I drove my own mother crazy.) They fall immediately into REM sleep, a light, active state of sleep that accounts for 50 to 90 percent of their sleep cycle and seems to regenerate psychic and emotional systems (as opposed to the deep, quiet, non-REM sleep that is largely responsible for physical regeneration). Very young infants can often sleep in bright light, strapped to your chest while you vacuum, in a car seat in a noisy restaurant, through a rousing church service, amid the roar of a stadium crowd, or in the realm of the screams of another baby. The baby's hormone levels, along with her inability to control fully the sleep-wake cycle, are among the reasons that a newborn baby will generally sleep every two hours but usually for no more than three to four hours at a time. It's a kind of physiological trial by fire for the parents, who have their own sleep-wake states radically reorganized by their infant's needs.

Ironically, unlike her exhausted parents, a newborn baby will tend to meet her need—and capacity—for sleep regardless of what the parents do. A baby will sleep when she needs to: in a car, in a parent's arms, in a swing. Then will come the day—and if you are lucky it might come around two months—when her stomach capacity has increased, her nervous system has begun to mature, and she will sleep for six, seven, maybe even eight hours at a time. Her body temperature will lower at night and rise by day, day/night periodicity will emerge, and adult sleep patterns will begin to be established. Your baby will no longer be quite so portable, but you should finally have some semblance of night and day returned to you.

In spite of the exhaustion, those first months passed in a steady stream of wonder. Maybe we were just too tired to do anything but stare, awestruck, or maybe our brains were just too dim to process anything more complicated than "wow," but Ella moved and we marveled that her body worked. As much as she was our child, she also seemed to be a kind of experiment conjured for our instruction. How did she work? What could she do? When would she begin to understand us? The world? Waking from a nap, for several minutes at a time she would remain in a curious, questioning state of grace. Quiet and alert, she gazed intently at the board books we held in front of her, her eyes tracking the pictures with movement as mysterious and unlikely as a divining rod's. A circle was as perplexing and new as a giraffe. We played music for her. Anything we liked: Brahms and Count Basie, Mozart, and Ella Mae Morse. She listened. We watched. Her mind captured changes in melody, pitch, pace, rhythm. Each new sound registered clearly by a startled glance, a widening of her eyes, a blink, a turn of the head, a furrowed brow. The world announced itself to her, and somehow she received it. Though she didn't understand, she comprehended or grasped something. This seemed to us both simple and unlikely. With milk and protection, her body sustained itself and grew. For many hours of the day I just stared at her, captivated. She was like a snake charmer and utterly unaware of her power.

For the first week Ella was profoundly content. Then she began to fuss. As our pediatrician had warned, the fussiness and crying continued to increase until she was six weeks old. At this point (just in time for her baptism) she was crying two to three hours a day. Most children fuss, defined as crying not clearly related to hunger, fatigue, or gas. Fussing is crying for crying's sake. Generally, fussiness emerges around the first week of life and peaks around week six. Some children may cry up to four hours in each twenty-four-hour period, and research suggests this kind of crying—different from and unrelated to colic—is not related to any external influence, nor to the environment, nor to gas, nor to poor caregiving. Instead, fussiness seems simply to reflect the immaturity of the nervous system, which is as yet unable to regulate states of consciousness and control environmental stimuli. In other words, we were stuck with it.

So every day, several times a day, there came a time when, tired of the books or her bouncy seat or being held, Ella would begin to squirm. Her reflexes would kick in and she would struggle against the swaddling (if such ineffective movements could really be called struggling). She would spit up and cry. Then we might take her for yet another walk in the stroller. Sometimes the fresh air would calm her, sometimes it wouldn't. No matter how fast or how slowly we walked, no matter how warmly we'd wrapped her (San Francisco is cold in June) nor how well we shielded her from the sun and wind, the fussing would mount until it reached a high-pitched crescendo and we were assaulted by that thin screaming, honking, caterwauling newborn cry. Nothing could make it stop, and it nearly undid me. As I walked with her I struggled to remain calm. If Kory was with me, we took turns pushing the stroller. Often, one of us would pick her up, but that did no good either. She just needed to cry, and I tried to avoid the pitying, perplexed, and downright judgmental stares of the other parents who strolled the path with their quiet, calm, sleeping babies. At home I would feed her (again and again) and Kory would pace the apartment, holding her against his shoulder. He would sit on the blue exercise ball and bounce her back to stillness, a drawn, stoic look on his face. Neither of us spoke much. Eventually she slept. Still, somehow, we remained enamored if exhausted. Most of our wardrobe was permanently stained with dark shadows of spit-up.

While it seems to the new parent that the infant is either asleep or awake, crying or not, infants actually cycle between six states of consciousness. There are two sleep states: active and passive; and four awake states: drowsy, quiet alert, active alert, and crying. In the quiet alert state the infant is calm, bright-faced, wide-eyed. She is relatively motionless but intensely attuned to her environment. In this state the infant is responsive to sight, sound, and touch. It is an optimal state for learning. In the active alert state the infant moves her limbs and her face. She is not so shining and wide-eyed, and she may be increasingly sensitive to noise, hunger, and fatigue. Her breathing may be slightly irregular. In this state she might fuss or cry. If you realize she is in this state, you might intervene and try to soothe her, to return her to a quiet alert state, then to drowsiness, then, eventually, to sleep.

It's possible, even likely, that Ella cried so hard because I didn't notice subtle changes in her state. I couldn't see that she had had enough and that soon it would be time for her to sleep. The best thing I could do would be to help ease her into a drowsy state. Some experienced mothers call this moment "catching the wave" or "finding the window," but it's a hard thing to do before you know your baby very well. Once you understand how your baby works, this rhythm becomes second nature. But no one can really teach it to you. It takes months of close and careful observation, years of experience, many trials and errors, and lots and lots of crying before most parents understand how their babies work, what all those movements mean, and what they can do about them.

The baby's cycling between states of consciousness happens more or less naturally, although each state has implications for caregiving. As you become more attuned to your child (Is she happy? Is she about to cry? Is her cry one of hunger or one of exhaustion?) you can help to soothe her before she learns to soothe herself. Then, as the central nervous system develops, these states become organized and are eventually controlled by the child. State organization is a crucial moment in development because it paves the way for the higher functions. This organization and modulation help the child to transition smoothly between sleeping and waking, to wake at appropriate intervals, to sustain uninterrupted sleep, to control sensory input, and to respond to the environment. All the books we were "reading" to her, all that walking, bouncing, feeding, and cooing, was our attempt to respond, very dumbly and blindly, to our daughter's cycling consciousness. Of course, we didn't know this at the time, and I'd guess few new parents do, but we had begun, as all parents do, to intuit something about our daughter's personality, something about her way of being in the world, something about how her consciousness and our own were beginning to meet and respond to each other, forming that chaotic, coherent rhythm of family life.

In the beginning, Ella's cries caused me physical pain. I thought I understood that she would cry for no reason, but I didn't, not really. In those early weeks, although Ella did not often cry hard, she cried persistently. It was a high-pitched crowing cry, like the cry of an angry cat, and it filled the apartment. It seemed to saturate my pores. Nothing could match the frustration and anxiety it provoked in me. In the late afternoon, during those eternally long hours between her last nap and Kory's arrival home, Ella was fretful and difficult to please. Where had my good-natured baby gone? What was wrong with me? While my mother was visiting, during the worst of these times, she would take Ella in her arms and walk with her. It wasn't so much that my mother could calm her and I could not, although this was certainly sometimes true. More important was the fact that Ella's cries didn't bother her. Ella cried and my mother held her. Ella cried and my mother calmly paced the apartment. Ella cried and my mother talked or sang or gently hushed her.

My mother was the unmoved mover who brought order and tranquility to my home.

"How can you stand it?" I finally asked.

"I raised three children, Lisa."

I knew this, of course. But I didn't, not really.

In the evenings, when Ella would not sleep, when it was too soon to feed her again and the hours between those earliest feedings seemed insurmountable stretches of time, Kory and I took turns trying to soothe her. Somehow Kory had discovered that she liked to be held tightly while he bounced slowly on the blue exercise ball. Sometimes this bouncing could calm her when nothing else would. In the evening, after dinner, we turned out the lights and kept the TV turned low. After an hour or so Ella would calm, her head would droop, her little eyelids would grow heavier with each pulse of the ball. Finally she would surrender to sleep. If we were lucky, she would remain asleep after we placed her in the bassinet. More often than not, as her head touched the mattress she would jerk awake and begin to scream. We would begin the routine again.

There is a theory of neurobehavioral organization, the Synactive Theory of Development, put forward by Heidelise Als, that posits a connection and interdependence between five major neurological subsystems that govern the infant's relationship to the world. These systems are independent and hierarchical, meaning that they mature one at a time, and each development is dependent on the successful organization of the prior system. They are also almost entirely dependent on the age of the child (measured from conception). For instance, in order to have state organization, the infant must first have an organized physiologic system, including cardiorespiratory and gastrointestinal systems as well as a motor system, which includes things like muscle tone and posture. Once this is achieved, the organization of the attentional/interactive system follows, which allows her to pay attention to her world and to sustain a well-defined period of alertness. This in turn enables her to self-regulate, to integrate and balance all of the other systems, and to actually modulate her states of consciousness. When all of these systems are organized and integrated the baby will be able to feed efficiently, coordinate sucking and swallowing, elicit responses from her caregiver, and console herself. She will also be able to control external stimuli and sensory input.

Als's theory is used primarily to inform caregiving practices and procedures for premature infants. By assessing developmental age alongside the biological and environmental needs of the infant, caregivers have been able to ensure better neurological outcomes. But, more broadly speaking, this model helps to explain to the lay person just how complicated infant consciousness is. There is a fundamental, necessary, and crucial pattern of neurological and physiological development that enables awareness, which is just that sense of being in the world that eventually makes us feel most human.

This precise pattern of development is one reason why, from a biological, developmental, and neurological perspective, birth is a transitional event for the baby rather than the decisive event it is for the parents. The most critical change for the new baby is the transition of her respiratory system—her lungs must learn to breath air almost immediately. (Her kidneys must also assume their function rapidly.) The moment of birth is not a developmentally significant one per se: the brain and nervous system don't suddenly "turn on" at birth. After all that trauma to me, when Ella emerged she hadn't changed in any fundamental way, certainly not in the physical, biological way that I had. Her change would come, certainly, as she learned to suck, tasted colustrum (then milk), felt something more than fluid against her skin, got used to gravity, regulated her own body temperature, and controlled her limbs. But, really, she possessed little more ability to cope with the world than she possessed the day before. The really interesting and significant changes would happen in the months after birth: the first smile, the first understanding and awareness of caregivers, the ability to call to them, the ability to grab for what she wanted. Only then, as her consciousness slowly coordinated, emerging from darkness and impulse and she began to act and look more like a baby and less like a thing from another world, only then did the real and really interesting changes begin. Until then, it remained entirely our responsibility to nourish, transport, sustain, and protect her. Obviously this was much more difficult to accomplish when she was outside my body rather than inside it. Compared to taking care of a newborn, pregnancy was a walk in the park.

Just past Ella's two-month "birthday," I was lying on the couch reading when I heard an awkward chortle from my daughter's room. Kory was changing her, and she was laughing. It was a halting laugh, more a gulp and guffaw, as though she were testing her voice and its capacity. It was primitive and graceless, but it was an unmistakable sound of glee.

And just like that, overnight, our morning routine changed. When we entered her bedroom she turned to us and smiled. It was clear that we were familiar to her. With her mobile rotating above her, she would stare and smile, tracking her favorite orange disc as it made its slow orbit above her head. We had discovered by accident that she was captivated by the wooden sculpture of the cow jumping over the moon that hung on her wall. For minutes on end she would stare and smile at its simple silhouette. It calmed her when she was crying and made her smile when she was quiet. There was also the business of the dog, one of those impossibly soft plush toys that friends can't help buying and new parents can't resist throwing in the crib. It was nearly as long as she. We'd lay it on her belly and she'd laugh, overcome with pure, libidinal pleasure. Then Kory discovered the simple act of seeing the dog hovering over her was enough to elicit the giggle. He tested her again and again, putting the dog away, bringing it back. Whether it touched her belly or not she'd wriggle and squirm in glee. She had no words, understood not a single syllable of language, but there it was: causality, thought, response.

One day, as I was putting laundry away in her room, I watched her watching me. She was planted in the middle of the room, supported by her exersaucer, a round, spaceship-shaped contraption with all manner of farm-themed manipulative toys affixed to its rim. The basket that held her upright swiveled so she could turn to face any corner of the room she liked. Mostly she sucked on and poked at the plastic toys, and this entertained her for long periods of time. As I tracked across the room and back, her eyes followed me. I turned to the drawers and back, stepped into the closet and out. Quiet and curious, her eyes never left me. I walked out of the room and then, hidden from her sight, turned around. There she was, her head turned to the door, watching for me, waiting patiently. When I entered the room, she smiled. I began to understand "mother," its permanence fixed to me like a shadow.

Mornings, Kory would bring her to me. As he laid her beside me, she would lunge and roll to her side, her mouth agape, latching on with practiced swiftness. She ate determinedly, greedily, and when she was finished, I would prop her on my knees, coffee in one hand, book in another, and we would read. Certain books and all animal sounds delighted her. She was knowledge, revealed to me in its most raw form. In the single, simple light of her understanding, we caught a glimpse of the most fundamental truth of our conscious nature: it is not the "what" that possessed us, but rather the "how." It didn't matter that much what she knew or what she could or couldn't do. None of the early development was remarkable in and of itself, none of it was especially distinguished. We parents are often mistaken in these early months: I knew one mother who believed her baby "advanced" because she could put a foot in her mouth at several weeks of age. There is, of course, something remarkable about babies, but it's not the *what*, it's the *how*, as in, "*How does she know how to do that?*" or "How did *that* happen?" It's easy to mistake development for achievement. But really, it's the very fact of knowledge—the fact that something, *anything* can be known—that's the remarkable thing. It was every bit as uncanny as her existence.

Very soon, like every other normally developing child, Ella discovered her hands and feet, laughed at her fingers in front of her face, stuffed four or five toes in her mouth in delight. Then one day, long before she could stand or even sit properly on her own, she recognized herself in the mirror. I held her in front of me, her arms waving, her feet dangling astride my leg, and she smiled at her image. She looked, she recognized, and she smiled. She understood that she was seeing herself, and that she was a thing separate from me. It would be months before she would know her name or respond to it, but there she sat, wriggling and laughing, and gazing quietly at the mirror, utterly self-possessed, possessed by her burgeoning self.

Jacques Lacan, the French psychoanalytic theorist, called this moment and this stage of being the mirror stage. It is the moment when the child—"though outdone by the chimpanzee in instrumental intelligence"—can recognize his image in the mirror as a reduplication of itself. She can wave her arms and understand that the waving arms belong to her. It is, Lacan writes, the moment of "jubilant assumption" of identity. It is the moment when the child perceives a certain unity of self, when she understands her self as distinct from her mother's self, and this moment of recognition paves the way for the higher functions of consciousness, for the symbolic sense of the self in the world. The child psychiatrist Margaret Mahler puts it another way: it is the moment when the child moves, finally, into a world populated by others. From the autonomous, symbiotic dependency of early infancy the child begins to understand that others are not merely extensions of her body. She has a body, and so do others, and the two are separate and distinct.

Although it would be many, many months before I would be able to inhabit a space apart from her and remember a self distinct from my motherhood, Ella had already begun the process. She was hatching.

On September 11, 2002, we woke to her squeals. I entered her room, which was flooded with morning light. As if the world were beginning anew, she sighed, and smiled, and squealed again. Her arms and legs flailed in joy with as much control as she could muster. It was as if I had appeared to her out of the darkness, a person she remembered but did not yet expect would appear. I stood over her crib and watched her track her mobile, transported with delight, and I thought *It has taken a year to make this baby, from embryo to infant.*

In three short months my horizon had shrunk, its farthest reaches now delimited by my baby's body. In her very ordinary activity was all the world worth attending. She learned to reach for toys, to tripod with her hands splayed between two legs, and then to sit independently. With her tiny mouth she cooed, sang, and spat out gutturals and other syllabic nonsense. She learned to roll from back to front and then, with great effort, from front to back. Daily we walked along the beach, as I had before she arrived, but now my gaze was lowered, fixed on the tiny, pulsing form below me. The horizon had never seemed so near, nor had it ever been so obscured. All of my dreams, my energy, were poured into her, and when I lifted my gaze, after many weeks, I realized how much of the world was outside of her. Yet, somehow, I didn't care. With the pull of a small planet, Ella had drawn the world into her. I was merely her satellite, content with the finite track of my orbit, its infinite rotations.

SEA CHANGE

For six months after Ella's birth my brain refused to work. It functioned haltingly, shifted gears with great difficulty, and many times simply refused to think about anything but my daughter. What I thought were my well-tuned intellectual pathways froze not through mis- or overuse but through some deliberate and nasty hormonal trick. The entirety of my mind was devoted to Ella, and it dwelt on her ferociously. The dexterity I had once had with ideas I now applied to figuring out her life. Instead of dwelling on Hawthorne's reinvention of the novel I watched Ella invent new ways to propel herself across the floor. The questions I pondered were no longer speculative, but consequential: not Why does Isabel Archer defy her aunt? but When will Ella learn that "no" is not a game? Not, How is sleep a metaphor in *The Blithedale Romance*? but, How do I get my daughter to sleep?

All of this made teaching and writing difficult. For the first weeks of the semester the disjunction between my life and my work was nearly unbearable. It took herculean effort to begin each seminar, leaving behind the long, tired, endlessly slow and nonverbal days and plunge into the heart of a book. While I don't think my students suspected the cause—not knowing any other me but the slow me—it usually took me the better part of the first hour before I felt fully present to them or to the book.

No longer did my life revolve singularly around the small orbit of my self. This is another cliché and the essential truth of motherhood: my world was my daughter. At six months I understood fully that I would always be Ella's mother. She would see me first and forever as her mother, and I would never, ever assume an identity so important to her as that one. The little girl in the park who told me her mother's name was "Mommy" had it right: if her mother had a name beyond that one, what did it matter to her?

As the months passed, I understood that Ella's claims on me were not just physical, but mental and emotional. Aches, soreness, tightness, the return of sciatic pain in my back and hip, these all reminded me that there would be no physical rest. Worse was the realization that, when Ella was seven months old and sleeping through the night, my own sleep was no longer restoring me. My physical exhaustion was merely a symptom of a much deeper, more pervasive and insidious fatigue. One Friday night, Kory arrived home from work to find me lying in bed, half-watching the television. I refused to speak in full sentences, refused to cook dinner; he served me leftovers, in bed, in my pajamas. We ate without talking. I was a slug: no mind, no motion, my life reduced to a primitive plodding through the necessary hours of the day. Although the weekend had arrived, it promised me no break, no release from the work of the week. I understood then that motherhood was a test of endurance. I could not have understood before then, before that very moment, the psychic and emotional toll motherhood exacted. It was not so much any one thing: the diapers, the crying, the sleeplessness, the new aches that came with each growth spurt, the feeding, the teaching—the endless teaching and repetition. Taken alone each of these tasks was tolerable. But they added up, so that the sum far exceeded the parts and I felt burdened beyond imagining with the small things of life. Claim after claim was made on me and on my time, and while I would often thrive on giving myself over to Ella, each and every day, if I was not very, very careful another piece of myself was lost to her.

All of my new-mother friends reacted differently to the burdens and realizations of these early months, when the monotony and miniaturization of motherhood became patently clear. One mourned the loss of her single life: being able to go where she wanted, when she wanted. Another had trouble adjusting to the radical new vision of herself required by motherhood. "I always thought I would travel," she confided. "I thought my life would always allow me to pick up and go, at a moment's notice." One struggled to succeed in her career—which she now practiced part-time—and in her motherhood. And another confessed to feeling imprisoned by her son, his need for naps. "I want to be out in the afternoons," she said. *Yes*, I thought, *of course*. For us, life no longer consisted of "I" statements, not really. For the time being our children would begin and end our thoughts and sentences. If we dared to begin a sentence with "I," we were bound to be disappointed, our syntax would be interrupted by the specter of the baby, who intruded always and everywhere. Even on my birthday, which I spent at a spa being soaked and steamed and massaged, my mind was full of Ella. She hovered there, larger than life, like life itself.

In these later months I understood viscerally, as if for the first time, Edna Pontellier's claim in *The Awakening* that for her little ones she would sacrifice her life but not her self. It is perhaps the essential and abiding truth of Kate Chopin's classic novel of motherhood and female independence, and also its unbearable wisdom. As surely as you would die for your child, in motherhood you will struggle to keep your self alive. A very young child will define your actions, circumscribe your space, limit and determine your thought. As the outward manifestations of your life are changed beyond recognition, so too is your inner landscape transformed by a fierce and selfless love. So riveting is this love, so addictive, that at first you may not notice that you have become undone, that you have crawled into a cavern so dark you cannot tell your hand from your child's or distinguish her heart from yours. Even upon noticing you may not care. If you are lucky, a remnant of your former self will remain to be returned to you many months, perhaps years later, like a piece of cloth from a favorite dress. From this notion you may recall a pattern, construct a new garment. You may find this new self better (hopefully you will find it no worse), but certainly you will find it different.

Motherhood is a role that you can never truly throw off, not even with death. For what child will think *The writer who was my mother is gone?* You hope she will think *My mother, who was a writer, is gone.* I might be Ella's mother who writes, who teaches, who dances, but first and always I will be her mother. The other things may be interesting but they are not very important additions to the equation. To argue that I am a better mother—or a particular kind of mother—because of my writing, my teaching, my passions and idiosyncrasies simply begs the question. We children may be very proud of what our mothers do. We may admire and aspire to their success (just as surely as we are determined to avoid their failures) but we care mostly, perhaps only, about the fact of, the concrete reality of, their motherhood.

I don't think that my daughter will care that I walked through the spring rain in Princeton, in love, poems blossoming in my mind. Nor that I hiked a precipitous path to the summit of Slieve

League, clung to the cliff and gazed down in terror and awe at the Irish Sea, taking measure of the very height and depth of the sublime. Nor will she care that many decades ago I sat in the fork of an old crabapple tree and read books to my baby brother. I may tell her that I danced with her father in a cave in Paris or drank gin with my best friend 110 stories above the world, in a tower that has been destroyed. None of these things will directly concern her. They are incidental, all those parts of my life beyond and before her. Though they have made me, they will make her only indirectly. I will not blame her, of course, for this oversight. For what role, what profession, what experience will ever overshadow the one I assume toward her? Other mothers, those who have survived this battle between the singular self and the doubling of life that occurs with motherhood—those who have made peace with the chaos as well as the wonder of it, who have come to understand themselves inside and outside their maternity—these are the women who take me aside and whisper conspiratorially, "It is the best thing I have ever done." Whether this is said with guilt or pride, awe or humility, I am never sure.

Now, understanding, my heart aches for my mother. To understand her as one thing only, to love her so fiercely for that one thing—when, like me, she had all that life beyond us . . . What arrogance is it that makes children believe their mothers have existed only and ever in their lifetime? This is the crisis of motherhood and its central sacrifice. Mothers—especially new mothers—experience viscerally the extreme limits and dangers of love, that dilemma so chillingly expressed by Emily Dickinson who, though childless, wrote more presciently than any other of the dilemma and danger of love:

> The Drop, that wrestles in the Sea—
> Forgets her own locality—
> As I—toward Thee

If we are unlucky or unfathomed, like Edna Pontellier, we are drowned. If we are strong and lucky, the struggle will return us to ourselves, sea changed. In those early months I felt often as if I were swimming underwater and holding my breath, and although my love for my daughter was fierce and redemptive and my husband was, by all the standards of new fathers, fantastically supportive and readily involved in taking care of her every need, still, even then, it was not at all clear to me that I would ever find my way back to dry land.

IN THE DARK

Often I woke in the middle of the night afraid of death. Around me, the night was black, blank, and filled with loss. As I lay still and cold, one moment after the next filled with bottomless grief. The world seemed full of endings. Though Kory slumbered next to me, I was conscious of only two others: my daughter asleep in the next room and my mother asleep, three thousand miles away. From the bottom of that well, I longed for only one thing: to bring them together.

Motherhood made me long for my mother as I had not since I was a child. Nights, after Ella had gone to bed and I had enjoyed long hours without her, my arms often felt empty not just for my daughter but for my mother as well. I wanted to hold her and say, "Now I understand." But the import of what I now understood could not be put into words. I felt it obliquely, as a keen longing. It had something to do with the circumstances of Ella's conception and with my grandmother's death. We had not named her after Lucy but there she was: *lux*, a light, just the same, poised between darknesses like Sylvia Plath's candle: "O love, how did you get here?"

For months my greatest fear was not that Ella would die but that I would. I was racked with terror at the thought of leaving her behind, motherless. I was terrified I would betray her in this way, and then who would look out for her? Day in and day out, who would care for her? Who would love her as I did? It was horrible, to be taxed with this worry on top of all the sleepless nights, the feelings of inadequacy, the general confusion that attends new mothers. I don't quite know why I felt Kory would not be enough for her, why I didn't believe that he could take over if I were to die. Maybe this was selfish of me, a moment of supreme ego. But Kory had not devoted his life to her, not in quite the same way I had. It wasn't that he wouldn't or couldn't (because he would and he could) but simply that he hadn't.

One day I voiced my fear to a friend, and she replied, "I know! Me too!" Then she confided that she and her husband had vowed to book separate flights were they ever to travel together without the children. She swore that she had friends who already did this. She told me that she knew others who avoided long trips in the car without the children. Then she confessed: she was afraid someone would steal her daughter—even while she was securely strapped into her car carrier seat. Obviously our fears were absurd. There was no more likelihood that we would die of a freak event now than before we had children. But the consequences of our deaths were now patently clear: we mattered in a way that we hadn't mattered before, not to ourselves, not to our parents, not even to our spouses. It must have been a primal instinct, or an outgrowth of the lizard brain, this acute sensitivity we had to danger and the possibility of death. We were more aware, not just of our children but of everything that life threw in our way.

One Sunday there emerged a new dimension to my understanding of my grandmother's death. For the first time I thought not of my mother, but of Catherine. As she lay on the couch that Sunday morning, did she know she was dying? Did she understand that her life was nearly over? That in a few short hours she would abandon her daughter? I thought she must have suspected something. For a body to break so quickly, so unexpectedly, over the course of a day, I imagine there must have been signs of the grave changes taking place within. I thought that she knew and I projected not only my mother's loss, as I had been imagining it for more than two decades, but my grandmother's own sense of helplessness and her absolute grief.

Though it was uncomfortable, it was inevitable that my thoughts returned to death. Being so close to birth, and being on such intimate terms with its freshness, I continued to confront that other mystery too. Having known that first delivery, I knew there would be another, for no one is vouchsafed two miracles. Between those two moments there was life, which at times seemed now a slow slope toward death. Ella would grow and change but each moment of her life knit her more tightly to her own mortality. I didn't dwell on this fact as fear, nor did I experience it as morbidity. It was simply something I reckoned with extraordinary clarity. Suddenly and at once I saw life in another dimension. I wondered when growing or aging—which was really just another name for the same thing—stopped bringing you into life and started bringing you out of it.

Motherhood made me familiar with this mortal creep of time. As surely as Ella was born, as surely as she might thrive, both she and I would one day cease. It was a sort of miracle to be able to hold these two moments—of life, of death—in mind at once; to be acutely conscious of both the present and of the presence and nearness of loss; to hold in my arms the evidence of life and death, for that is what my daughter was: an inspired, poetic fact. She gave me an accidental genius, and if it filled me with night terrors, it also filled me with song. Of course, I could not function like this forever. No one can, and remain sane. I could not even function like this when I was awake in the safe daylight hours. I confronted the night, made good note of it, then I put the paralyzing terror from my mind. I held it at bay by talking constantly to my mother, by sending her fat folders of pictures and envelopes packed with videotapes. Ella and I flew east to visit her, and she and my father came frequently to California. If the crisis was an existential one, the remedy for it was pragmatic: we forged new ties with each other, with life.

This deep knowledge, this embrace of death, became the source of my fiercest love. Maybe all of us carry this knowledge in our bones. If so, it should make us love more and better, more truly, more generously. But we have fallen. We sin not in gaining this intimate knowledge of life and death but because, once gaining it, we forget it so soon and so entirely.

OUT OF
THE BODY

For Easter my parents flew across the country for a visit. Ella would turn one in just two months, and I had settled into a busy routine of writing, teaching, and mothering. There were many claims on my time, some of which I was just beginning to understand. Preparing for the holiday created others.

On Good Friday, the night on which Christians commemorate Christ's suffering and death on the cross, I was running late. My parents went on to church ahead of me, and when Kory arrived home, I rushed to join them. By the time I arrived at the old mission chapel, a small structure adjacent to the basilica where the English-speaking congregants gathered to begin their service, the church was full. I seated myself in the last row, among strangers. My parents were many rows ahead of me, so I sat alone through the first prayers. Being alone, even among strangers, was not a state to which I was accustomed in those days. Between Ella and Kory, my students, and the housekeeping, my days were busy and full and my mind was in a constant state of chatter. Quiet. Solitude. Peace: these were things that had disappeared from my life.

That evening, the chapel was dim and hushed. The adobe walls were cool and white. The voices of the choir surrounded me, tenors and baritones rising in sober song. I wasn't alone, but I was suddenly mindful of the fact that my mind as well as my body was still. The steady chanting comforted me. My mind emptied. I breathed.

I was raised Roman Catholic, attended Mass regularly as a child, and received the usual sacraments. Faith has always been present in my life, but it has never been easy. My relationship to the Church has sometimes been rocky; it has often been critical. It is not easy for me to reconcile many of my beliefs about equality, sexuality, and the role of women and women's rights with Church doctrine. It is not easy to be Christian in the secular academic world. It is not easy to overlook the corruption and scandal that have infected the Church. For a long time, I avoided Catholicism without wholly giving up on spirituality. When we married, I returned, supported in part by the teaching of the brilliant, compassionate, socially conscious pastor who married Kory and me and who later baptized Ella. I found something unavoidable in the rituals of the Mass and the ceremony of the sacraments. They were beautiful and familiar, or perhaps I found them beautiful in their familiarity. They were the vehicle for how I learned to believe and they were finally how I chose to continue my belief. They returned my distracted mind to what was right and to what must be righted, to what was necessary and what was good. When, of course, I promptly forgot all of these things in the midst of the noise and chaos of a busy work and family life, I found that Mass could ground me. On very rare occasions it had proved to be something more.

On that Friday, the English- and Spanish-speaking congregations were to celebrate a joint service, so we processed from the smaller mission to the much larger, grander basilica, to join a half dozen clergy and nearly a thousand congregants for the Veneration of the Cross. Like all Good Friday services, this one was long and austere. The church was dim and bare, stripped of all ornament. There was no music save the dirgelike chanting. I felt as far from redemption as it was possible to be. We chanted and prayed in Spanish and English, then prayed and chanted some more. Old women worried their rosary beads. As if sensing the night's seriousness, even the youngest children sat obediently still.

Near the end of the service a wooden cross large enough to crucify a small man was borne down from the altar and passed overhead through the pews, hand over hand, to be venerated. Some simply touched it, others kissed the crude wood. Now, as we confronted it, the cross became more than aesthetic icon; the bulk and weight of it added up to a kind of fact, a real thing at the bedrock of belief. As the cross passed slowly from congregant to congregant I watched and considered what the cross was—not simply what it symbolized. I watched and tried unsuccessfully to ignore the fact, both specific and general, of torture and extremely painful death. I watched the cross carried through the basilica, borne awkwardly like a boat on a rocky sea. I watched as it approached me rising and falling on the tide of arms. Steadily, it moved closer until it was upon my father, then me, and we carried it over our heads. It was rough and heavy, as profane as it was sacred. Being underneath it, it was not enough simply to touch it and let it pass on. For a moment I was forced to bear the cross's weight, and as it bore down on me, as I passed it along the crowded pew, even as it passed away from me there was in that moment, a moment out of time. A pause in my life and something strange possessed me. I felt an unexpected tremor. Then it passed. Something had visited me. It came, imparted, and was gone. I stood there, all awonder. I was not changed so much as infused.

The first time I felt such presence directly I was sixteen and camping in Yosemite with a friend and her family when we were hit by a storm with powerful, crashing rains and gale-force winds. The noise was terrifying, and our tent shook and bent under its force. It was too late and too dark to break camp, and certainly too dangerous to drive back down the mountain. So we huddled in the tent, unable to sleep. We circled around the lantern, and they, being devout Christians, did what they knew best: we prayed. Having never prayed with my family outside of church, or on any occasion away from the dinner table, the experience was strange and new, and slightly embarrassing. I was scared, and we were entombed in that tent, and so I prayed with them. Even as the storm raged outside, calm descended inside the tent. We were safe, implausibly and unreasonably safe. I knew this, but I knew something else, too. It was the first time I understood an intimacy with spirit, a feeling I was not to know again with such certainty for twenty years, not until I bore that cross over my head and into the arms of the next worshipper.

After the service the congregation processed through the streets. Many western Catholic cultures have some version of this procession, which is meant to symbolize the way of the cross or to reenact the drama of the crucifixion. First went the cross, shouldered by several men. Behind it four men carried a life-sized bier on which an effigy of the dead Christ was shrouded and bedecked with flowers. Behind him followed a life-sized statue of Mary in mourning robes, a golden halo encircling her head. Behind her, more than a dozen purple and white Easter banners depicted the central Easter symbols: a dove, a cross, the cup, the lamb. We carried candles and many sang somberly in Spanish. We walked slowly. The windows above the street were filled with people who peered down at us. I saw them perched behind bay windows, balancing wine glasses and dinner plates. I thought about my daughter and husband at home, and my own parents who walked close to my side. I thought of the joy of Easter that would dawn in a day. I gazed on Mary's pale face, her eyes large and dark. Staring at her frozen form, I was hollowed by grief. I understood newly the passion of Easter: not just to lose your child, but to see him murdered. What would it matter that your child was God? At Mission Dolores, my parish now, or at Our Lady of Sorrows, my childhood parish, I had never once understood what it meant to worship under her auspices.

On Easter morning the basilica bloomed with white lilies and gold fabric draped the pulpit. A luminous white banner obscured the crucifix. Candles flanked the altar and sacristy, and to the right of the nave the baptismal font gently lapped. Water, light, white and gold. Surrounded by these simple symbols, my heart sang.

As if knowing my mind that morning, the priest, in his homily, addressed the tension between the physical and the spiritual. Mary Magdalene and the others, he said, went to the tomb to do a good work. They were there for an ordinary ceremony, to tend to the dead. They found a theophany—the presence of God. Instead of the pedestrian, an impenetrable mystery. In the place of the domestic, a divine revelation. It is this single impossible event that stands at the heart of Easter, indeed of all Christianity.

For this joy, Easter has long been my favorite holiday. Far surpassing the joy of nativity that comes at Christmas, Easter is the joy of rebirth, of second coming, of renewal. Like the diurnal or the yearly cycle, the Easter cycle reminds us that if we are able to look a certain way, there is no end, only new beginnings. Not just eternal sorrow but always new joys. It is a resurrection of spirit and of soul, but it is also one of body. This, perhaps, is the mystery and power of Easter and its central paradox: only through death can there be rebirth; only through the body does the spirit transcend.

This deep spiritual knowledge—of transcendence, of transformation—is not unlike maternal knowledge. It not so different from the mother's knowledge of the nearness of birth to death—her own, her child's—or from her own thunderous undoing in labor. There is something else, something in bearing and birthing and rearing our babies that, like Sylvia Plath's mythical Ariel, hauls us through air until we emerge raw and transformed in a place undreamt, to a self undone, to a knowledge utterly strange and new and, perhaps, a little bit frightening. Certainly it was through the very most common and ordinary experiences of my maternal body, through the physiological changes of pregnancy, the violence of birth, the tedium and joy of nursing, that I had often found a place of astonishing unspoken revelation.

I knew other women sometimes experienced similar epiphanies. My sister had remarked to me, "That's how you know there has to be a God. That a microscopic egg and microscopic sperm can come together and form something so complicated is just a miracle." Michelle had once stopped herself in the middle of one of our early, endless discussions about fetal development. "You study and study," she confided, "and you learn all the processes and read all the books. And then when you see the baby come out, you step back and take off your medical goggles and think 'oh my God.' That's what made me start going to church again."

That Easter morning Handel's "Halleluiah Chorus" rang through the basilica, horns and tympanis heralding such joy as is promised by the Easter transformation but which is so rarely realized. I remembered suddenly that same moment the year before when Ella, snug in my womb, had stirred at its strains. My soul had strained at her stirring and I began to cry. Whether moved by hormones or some more ephemeral influence, I could not discern. But now I understood whether God moved me or whether it was only the effect of my body and its most ordinary pregnancy—this distinction hardly mattered. Something had vaulted me out of my pedestrian practice of faith, startled me beyond intellect, past reason and routine, and I understood. Spirit, body, the spirit in the body . . . they were all the same ordinary thing, the same veritable theophany.

AN AMERICAN
WOMAN'S HOME

Like all mothers, I learned on the job. Through trial and error I figured out how to take care of my daughter, how to entertain her, and how to keep myself showered, mostly rested, and somewhat sane. I relied more rather than less on intuition and on daily consultations with family, friends, books, the Internet. Motherhood was a puzzle whose pieces I studied intently so that slowly, hour after hour, day after day, the pieces began to fit together. We established a routine of sleeping, feeding, playing, soothing, sleeping . . . We found places that pleased us both: mom/baby yoga; long walks around Stowe Lake in Golden Gate Park, where there were always ducks and turtles to feed; a playgroup in a local church basement that housed sufficient apparatus to entertain Ella on rainy days; library story times; bookstores; the beach; the zoo. I slept when she slept, I wrote when she slept and I read often, to Ella and for myself.

It is true that many new mothers suffer from postpartum depression and that the act of having a baby can alter your chemistry so severely that you are no longer able to cope with your life, certainly not with your baby. But it is also true that motherhood can bring an uncanny, unexpected joy. Later I came to know mothers who had struggled with mental illness and depression all of their lives and who, after the birth of their children, were able to maintain a period of happiness and placidity for up to a year without the medication they had always relied on. For them new motherhood offered a temporary reprieve, but a real one.

Part of my own elation was certainly due to the hormones that flooded my body. It was also due to the fact that motherhood had, in fact, made me slow down. It made me live in the present. It forced me to focus not simply on my daughter but on the rest of the things that mattered to me. It made me jettison everything extraneous from my life, so that what was left were the things that were real: my daughter, my husband, our home, my books, teaching, writing. It made me selfish with my time. I said no to activities that might be stressful. I said no to extra housework. I learned quickly how to prioritize and how to conserve energy. Call it self-preservation, or call it selfishness—or attribute it to the academic training that had taught me the reward of focused, solitary hours—but those early months of motherhood proved on balance to be productive and beneficent. There were challenges to my independence, and the weariness, of course, and the confusion about who, exactly, I was becoming, but these moments were quickly folded into a life punctuated daily by little epiphanies of joy. Ella sat up, she smiled at me, she began to creep across the floor like a sniper, she laughed and cuddled, she waved, she babbled, she slurped down new foods, she rolled and clung to me or Kory, she learned new things every day. If I stopped and looked at the world from her point of view and considered everything she had to learn about it, it was enormously interesting. She was interesting. So while I saw some new mothers struggling with the daily chores of motherhood, their lives bordering on misery, I wondered, with more than a little arrogance, what was wrong with me. Why wasn't it harder? Nine months passed like this.

Then one day everything changed.

I would like to say that the change was gradual, a slow awakening to a new kind of difficulty, but it was not. One day it was easy, and the next it was not.

It was a close, gray morning, the kind of day peculiar to certain parts of San Francisco where the sky hangs low and radiates a dull, dirty white light and the air is saturated with an unpleasant, humid chill, like a damp dishcloth. It was the kind of day that made it difficult to remember the month or the season of year. Yet as Ella and I made our way to playgroup, I felt none of the oppression usually brought on by the low clouds and dim light. Outside, the world was dingy, but my small world still sung with promise.

Overnight, it seemed, Ella had become a little girl. Her features, once soft and round as her favorite polar bear, began to take shape. Her golden hair had filled with highlights. Her eyes radiated intelligence and understanding. She questioned me, palms open to the sky, a quizzical shrug to her shoulder, a rising pitch to her voice. She pointed at things she wanted: her puppy, a pinwheel, the remote control. She clapped and bounced, but only to music that pleased her. She knew the names of most of the things in her world.

After playgroup that morning, after I had sat in that basement—which up to that point had been a fulfilling, companionable place to spend a few social hours—after I had listened to the endless litany of where Cheerios were on sale, what brand of diapers worked better on which gender, how many activities a particular nine-month old baby could accomplish in one day, how expertly another's "swimming" lessons were going, why one mother took such pride in not finding the time to shower,

or how another hadn't put her baby down for a nap *ever* . . .
after the storm of all that nothing, I found myself undone.

I craved adult companionship. Desperately, I craved a friend
whose experiences paralleled my own, one who inhabited the
shadow world of motherhood but who was not consumed by
its drudgery. My friends from pregnancy had all returned to
work or moved out of the city. I was alone, and I understood
for the first time, with absolute clarity, why women went mad.
I understood why Edna Pontellier drowned herself.

It was not the children. I doubted that it had ever been the
children. Rather, it was the life that they required; it was everything that surrounded and supported them. It was other mothers, of which I was certainly one. That afternoon, as soon as
Ella lay down in her crib, I, too, sought the comfort of deep,
oblivious sleep.

When I woke I understood more specifically that what was
hard about mothering my baby wasn't really the sleeplessness,
the poop, the spit-up, the mess at mealtimes, the carrying, or
the soothing. Nor was it her generally noisy, demanding nature. These things were challenging but in the end they were
the simplest things about having a child. What finally unwound
me was the repetitive, isolated nature of these chores. I did the
same things, over and over and over. I did them alone, without
company or conversation. Once they were done, they had to be
done again. And when I went out to be with other mothers, we
talked about nothing else. I knew there was more, much more,
to motherhood, but that afternoon it seemed to consist only of
endless mundanity. My life had been reduced to my baby's. If
motherhood was joy, it was no less tedious.

I understood why the Victorians hired nurses, why they raised
their children in separate wings, and why the profession of caregivers was indispensable to creating the life of leisure so sought
after and so highly prized by the rising middle class. I understood
why my contemporaries—even those who didn't work—hired

nannies and babysitters to watch their children. I understood why my sister declaimed with a force unusual for her, "It's much easier to go back to work." All of my years of feminism and women's studies, all that theory was embodied and made urgently real by my little child, by my messy, exhausted life, by the other mothers. No one cared about us. I wasn't even sure that we cared about us.

In the mid-nineteenth century Catharine Beecher published a thick volume entitled *The American Woman's Home*. Nominally coauthored by her much more famous sister, Harriet Beecher Stowe, the book's stated purpose was to be a "Guide to the Formation and Maintenance of Economical, Healthful, Beautiful and Christian Homes." In the scope and significance the book awards to the life of the home, it essentially calls for a revolution in domestic arrangements. Granted, Beecher argues that the truest place for a woman is at home, tending to it and to her children. There is much talk in the book of heaven and of family life as heaven's truest reflection. But for a modern reader to see this philosophy as repressive and limiting is to ignore the truly radical kernel of Beecher's thought: "It is the aim of this volume to elevate both the honor and the remuneration of all employments that sustain the many difficult and varied duties of the family state, and thus to render each department of woman's profession as much desired and respected as are the most honored professions of men." Beecher offers advice on architecture and interior design; she presents floor plans and storage solutions, including a compelling labeling system; she designs fantastically modern-looking built-in cabinets and custom shelving for the closet, the pantry, and the laundry room. There are precise instructions for creating art and for constructing a Wardian Case, an ambitious indoor terrarium; plans for ventilating and heating, for potting and displaying all manner of plants; ideas for instilling manners in your children and spouse and creating healthful drinks (and who doesn't still need *those?*). In short, Beecher is interested in all things that make the home more healthful, more efficient, and more beautiful for the middle-class family. She makes the prescient, and still relevant, argument that the work of the family is not appreciated, that women are "not trained for these duties as men are trained for their trades and professions, and that, as the consequence, family labor is poorly done, poorly paid, and regarded as menial and disgraceful." *The American Woman's Home* aims to change all that.

Beecher's volume is a training manual, a handbook of affordable design and healthy living and a compendium of fitness, lifestyle, mothering, modern architecture and style advice. It approaches these promiscuous and varied domestic arts pragmatically, with more than a little attention to science. In this ambition, and in the seriousness with which the author tends to so-called and so-delegated women's work, that Beecher elevates its significance. For her, the home is the place where life begins and which sustains all moral and physical interaction in the public sphere. It is not refuge but foundation, not afterthought but preface, not an oasis from modern life but its primary source of sustenance.

Really, the book is a precursor to all the contemporary lifestyle magazines, TV talk shows, blogs, and Web sites that have reinvented the domestic arts for the post-millennial home (think: parenting advice and online communities, cooking how-to's, craft mavens, reality nanny shows, home makeover shows). For Beecher, the home and motherhood (its beating heart center) are not simply sentimental refuges from work; the home is a radical alternative to consumer culture, to the getting and spending and laying waste of our powers that consumed men and the rest of civilization. For her, the created home is a political act.

In my despairing months, by following some lost track of memory I was led back to Beecher's book, and the ideas that I had once dismissed—or not quite fully comprehended—were suddenly resolved. Like so many other things in the previous year, my politics had also been retooled by my maternity. I began to suspect that modern feminism had gotten it at least partly wrong. If our society were to be truly transformed, something along the lines of Beecher's vision should have been part of the platform. In devaluing the home and the vast range of domestic work—childrearing included—and in fighting a fight largely for the right to work outside the home, the modern feminist movement ignored a singular power already available to women and, maybe more important, to the collective cultural imagination. Rather than fighting to re-invent the home, or to effect a real transformation of values, or to legitimize and legalize the domestic and childrearing work that so many women engage in—which is necessary to support any mother's work outside the home—we have found it easier to map power where it already existed. Is this really my only choice? Between the intense demands of an academic career (supported by full-time childcare) and the mind-deadening contemplation of Cheerios?

Of course, I had benefited directly from the women's movement. My education, my travel, even the privilege I had to choose to stay home and raise my daughter while working part-time—all of this was certainly indebted to feminism's second wave. But how is this movement serving me now? And what comes next? I felt I belonged in neither world: much of my energy was invested in raising Ella so I couldn't fully claim my professional identity, but neither could I identify with what seemed to me to be the petty concerns of motherhood. I loved my daughter and I loved my home. I did not love the stay-at-home culture of mothering.

What does feminism offer my daughter? Would the major inheritance of her generation be the so-called mommy wars, where stay-at-home mothers argue with "working" mothers about the relative rightness of their choices and the value of their work? Would she get her education and launch a career only to struggle with the same impossible choice: to work or not to work? Would she, too, feel overwhelmed by the second shift that waited for her inside the home after a workday outside of it? Would she feel pervasive guilt if she turned her childrearing over to someone else (nanny, babysitter, daycare provider)? Would she feel a sinking dread when she realized that her education and career had been hijacked by a maternity that took her out of the workforce? Would she panic about the financial dependence that came with pursuing her career part time or not at all? Worst of all, when I contemplated where mothers had been and where we might go, I knew that this part of the debate was relevant only for those with enough money or education to make a choice in the first place. In the years to come, writers like Ann Crittenden and Caitlin Flanagan would write profoundly about the pressing political and moral issues surrounding women's work in and out of the home, and the moral and legal conundrums surrounding the choice to hire nannies, daycare providers, or housecleaners. When Ella was an infant one of my college students watched her on the nights that I taught, and our apartment was so small that the cleaning and the chores had not yet become a wedge in our marriage. Relieved of these pressing domestic issues in that first year, I understood the crisis and failure of feminism differently. To my mind, the women's movement hadn't really changed anyone's mind—mine included—about what was important in the home, nor why. Becoming a mother had suddenly shown me that the home and what happened in it mattered vitally. To my great surprise, Ella had taught me that all of it—pregnancy, motherhood, domestic life—was interesting. She had taught me that to work inside the home is a worthwhile occupation. But this realization left me in limbo, at great odds with my education and, really, with most of the professional working world. To them, I was hidden in plain sight.

There are many serious and important reasons to educate our

daughters so they are able to participate vitally and actively in public life and to establish a career before (or alongside) establishing home and family, however we come to define these in the future. The life of the mind—the arts, science, politics, medicine, business, service—is vital for our daughters. I cringed when a friend imagined her daughter's wedding or another spoke about her child's future husband. I had no such future in mind for my daughter, not then. Nor did I think for a moment that our mothers were wrong to fight the good fight or that the fight was anywhere near finished. I had challenged my undergraduates to claim feminism for themselves. I would teach my daughter to go out in the world, to cultivate a public voice, to create a space for herself, and to forge a career she could count on.

In the wake of my depression, in those gray days when motherhood seemed to be drowning me, I sensed something had been missing from the public dialogue. I was not unhappy in my home nor with my daughter, but I was deeply unhappy with what those facts made of me in—and to—the rest of the world. I asked myself daily, Why didn't motherhood matter? Why was the home still a separate, unequal sphere? Why were mothers and children still so isolated from those things that really mattered to the childless, to the world outside the home? Why did we talk endlessly about stupid things like Cheerios and diapers? Why did I feel so fractured?

That was how I knew that Beecher was right: the life of the home had to be remade. It could be defined broadly or narrowly, liberally or conservatively, but it had to matter in real and consequential ways. The home had to enter the cultural imagination as more than a repository for sentimental aspiration or political pandering. It had to be seen as a productive place, a fundamental social unit, a place of education, a generator of health, a source of pleasure, even a nurturer of invention and creativity. Certainly we should fight for more balanced work schedules, for greater support of childcare, for equitable paternity and maternity leave, for a saner work/life balance (including flex-time and more flexible sick leave). But in cultivating motherhood, indeed in cultivating all parenting as an invisible, lesser sphere— in refusing to politicize motherhood and the work of the home, in the long delay or downright denial of motherhood's value, in handing over the work of the home to cleaning services and the work of raising children to daycare workers, nannies, and professional educators—our feminist forerunners did us a disservice. In pushing women out the door, feminism helped make the family and the work of the family invisible. They diminished the significance of family work and how families work. And we post-feminists continue to fail ourselves, our daughters, our sons, our husbands, every parent, and the culture at large by not reimagining this sphere ourselves. I knew that every time I located my real life elsewhere, outside of the home and away from my family or at least extraneous to my daughter, I diminished myself and my daughter and the life we shared at home with my husband. Every time I felt trapped inside my home I knew the feminist culture that had reared me had failed me. Every time I felt left out or severed from my "working" friends, I experienced a critical failure of imagination. Every time I experienced motherhood as marginal I was blind to the fact that it had revolutionized every aspect of my life. Motherhood was a political act. Finally I came to believe that in its insistence on the home as an original, generative space, there was something astonishingly radical about nineteenth-century radical domesticity, something we have forgotten and would do well to remember. There is more to creating a domestic space and much more to mothering than wiping counters and counting Cheerios.

I knew, of course, that I could not effect a cultural change by myself. My realization did not propel me into a local political career, nor even into volunteering in some more public way. But I resolved not to be undone by the warring cultures in which I found myself. I would not grant my intellectual career primacy over my family, nor would I give it up wholly to sequester myself in the land of milk and honey-nut O's. I continued to move between my worlds of teaching, writing, and mothering, and I tried hard to see how each inflected the other. I tried not to value one over the other (though some days I certainly preferred one over the other). I worked hard at my courses. I made time in my life for my colleagues. I made time in my life for my writing. I brought Ella out into the world, all of the world at appropriate times (like libraries and bookstores, museums and restaurants), not just to spaces populated by other babies. I tried to remember what mothering was teaching me about immediacy and observation, patience and education. I learned not to anticipate and I tried to accept gracefully the slow pace of my career. I learned there was pleasure in the present as well as in striving for the future. I knew my daughter was learning things at an astonishing rate, and I resolved to pay attention to her. I resolved not to pander to the pettiness of maternal culture. Motherhood was taxing enough. To indulge in the culture's small-minded clutter of needs and consumption would be my death knell. If motherhood had reinvented me, I also saw that motherhood needed some reinventing, too.

After that gray day I struggled a long time to find like-minded friends and regular companions for myself and for Ella. There were many lonely days, many long talks with my mother and friends who lived across the country, many nights spent complaining to my husband. Eventually we moved closer to my husband's work, into a community with a more stable population of families and a vibrant walking culture. I found a diverse, close-knit group of women whose friendship nurtured me profoundly.

In the end I came to believe that the real cultural battle is not between mothers who work outside the home and those who do not. The real battle is between those who find the home interesting and those who do not, between those who understand its transformative work and those who do not. To make peace with my choice to work part time and still spend most of the hours of the day inside my home attending to my daughter and domestic concerns I had to believe that what happened inside my home was in every way equal to what happened outside. I had to confirm continually that what was inside my home could—and should—transform what happened outside. Over time I found that my greatest support would often come from parents who worked. Some worked full time, some part time, some were writers and artists, yes, but others were attorneys, journalists, and other professionals. What bound us together was not what we did inside or outside the home but the extent to which we allowed our children to reinvent us. It was not that we chose to have children nor that we stayed home full time nor that we worked. Work status in itself meant nothing. Instead I found my support in parents who felt similarly about the work of motherhood and the space of the home. What bound us together was the fact that we found our children interesting, that we were inspired by them, that we had allowed our lives to be changed by them.

It was not radical to go back to work nor was it radical to stay home. Nor was it especially innovative to work part time. Beecher was right: what is radical is remembering that domestic life matters. What is radical is allowing yourself to be transformed by your children, in insisting that the life of the home is imaginative work, and that it, too, can be reimagined.

FLYING HOME

In her eighth month Ella began to acquire language. Late one afternoon we sat together on the floor of her room with a dozen picture blocks scattered before us. She turned one block after another in her little hands, examining first a tiger, then an egg, then a hat or a zebra. She looked at them so intently that I asked her, "Where is the butterfly?" She looked at me then pointed to the block in front of her, which did, in fact, picture a butterfly. I moved the block and asked again, and then once more. Each time she sought the right block. I quickly discovered she knew the names of many things: puppy, bird, block, book, daddy, ball, duck, baby. One word at a time I would ask her for an object, and she would turn her gaze upon it, fix her eyes steadily, and smile. Sometimes she would point. That night she sat with her doll in the bath, her tiny finger exploring the even tinier nubs of her baby's eyes, nose, ears, and mouth. She was consumed by these particulars, by understanding the landscape of the face, the location of eye and ear; I, in turn, was consumed by her. A thrill possessed me. The day before she had seemed caged in unknowing. Now she understood.

As startling as those first verbal recognitions were, Ella's acquisition of language had, in fact, begun many months earlier. At the tail end of one long day, when she was four or five months old, Ella sat facing me in my lap. Having exhausted our repertoire of books, mobiles, music, and the play mat, I was back to making sounds: vowel sounds and consonant sounds and animal sounds. I ran through the music of language in the most primitive way. Yet that day, to my great surprise, she answered me. I crooned, she sighed. I hummed, she hissed. I crowed, she sputtered. It wasn't exactly language, but it was a basic social understanding. One speaks when one is spoken to. My turn, your turn. Call and response. However I chose to understand it, I knew that Ella had, inexplicably, figured something out. The moment startled me, for in those exchanges she had asserted a voice, one of the primal markers of identity, individuality, and independence. Her voice calling out to me was haunting; it was like seeing the ghost fly from the machine.

How and when these transformations had occurred remained as profound as the mystery of her life. Just as suddenly as her zygote had emerged, seemingly from nothingness, the spark of understanding flooded her mind. It was the most profound change to have overtaken her, and with it she assumed a new attitude toward the world. Always alert, now she seemed almost to have a sense of herself in the world. She seemed to sit straighter and to focus more intently. Things acquired names. She could touch her polar bear with purpose. She could give him to us or take him away. Knowing him newly, knowing his name, was a new kind of knowledge: it was power, and it offered her a kind of control.

A few evenings later, as I nursed her to sleep, I gazed down at her, remembering how she had once fit entirely in the small circle of my arms. Her pleasure there had been complete. Already

I could see that a kind of deep, unconscious pleasure had left her. She no longer settled herself into that surrendered position, but nursed quietly and briefly. Now, her larger pleasure was beyond me, in the world and its newness and in her own growing ability to communicate.

In the first year there are many things a child will learn. She will learn to grab, to shake her head, to bat with her hand at an object that tantalizes her—a hanging toy, perhaps, or a plush block. She will learn to roll, then to sit, then to crawl. She will pull herself to stand, then cruise along the furniture. Finally, she will walk. She will learn to suck, to chew, to hold a spoon and feed herself. She will learn to make sense of what she sees, hears, and touches. She will come to understand what is hot, what is dirty; how to climb up the stairs, how to climb down; how to push, how to pull; how to use a pincer grasp to pick up a tiny object expertly between two tiny fingers, how to shake a rattle; how to drink from a cup. With help she will learn to sleep alone in her crib, to comfort and soothe herself to sleep without breast, without bottle, and to wake at a relatively appropriate hour of the morning. The process seemed endless. Often, it seemed effortless.

I tried to remember to turn on music, to set her mobile in motion, to allow her to lie uninterrupted on her play mat with a butterfly and a caterpillar and a sun dangling above her. I took her out of the apartment so she would understand that the world was wider than my arms. I tried to name everything for her: diaper, washcloth, onesie, soap, crib, blanket, book. I read to her, over and over, letting her eyes behold the pages, though at first they were merely masses of color and unresolved shapes. In many ways my love for her was a kind of discipline; my most fundamental job was to teach her things about the world. Yet day after day I often found that it was she who exerted the more strenuous discipline; it was she who taught me daily how to teach her, she who taught me about myself and my limits, and the farthest reaches of love and endurance. In one of those strange illogical reversals that I came to accept as the terra firma of motherhood, I became my daughter's disciple.

Still, Ella's learning baffled me. How did she acquire knowledge of her capabilities and her world? Was she acquiring knowledge itself? Or was she simply acquiring the ways and means of knowing? Instinct told me that it had to be both, for as soon as she came to know things she also knew how to solve problems. She learned "chair" and also that many types of them existed. She learned to climb, and then used this skill to acquire objects out of reach. Like all children, she would drop something— from her crib, her high chair—and wait for us to retrieve it for her. Thus she learned about categories, about cause and effect, about consequence. In fact, Alison Gopnik, Andrew N. Meltzoff, and Patricia K. Kuhl have argued convincingly in *The Scientist in the Crib* that this model of learning accurately reflects a baby's way of being in the world. Babies, they propose, are like little scientists whose "theories" about the world are tested and revised by experience. We learn not by having material inscribed on the "blank slate" of the brain, but by having our innate and acquired knowledge challenged and reinforced by experience. One of our most profound evolutionary adaptations is that we are programmed to learn, and what Ella revealed to me daily was that learning is not simply passive and receptive, but active and reciprocal. That she could adapt my teachings to her own purposes simply reflected how learning is one of our most basic ways of being in the world.

In our earliest years this learning happens at an astounding rate, and this startling and rapid development is evident on the most basic physiological level. Though our brains possess at birth all of the neurons we will ever have in our lives, the synapses between them—the electrical connections or wiring that make thought and perception possible—are largely made after birth. This process, known as synaptogenesis, is one of furious growth in which dendrites and axons sprout and connect at the rate of nearly 2 million per second until age two. Such phenomenal growth comprises the exuberant period, during which the brain produces many more connections than it will eventually need. At age three a child's brain contains twice as many synapses as an adult's. Then, through experience, a kind of pruning occurs so that inactive synapses are eliminated and active ones are strengthened. Like that exuberant growth, pruning takes place on a similarly epic scale: nearly twenty billion synapses per day may be pruned between early childhood and adolescence. This process allows each child's brain to respond maximally to her own particular environment and to be highly attuned to (and tuned by) her own unique, lived experience. It is this complicated combination of biology and experience—nature and nurture—that allows us to be flexible and creative learners and enables us to adapt, grow, and change. And if this exuberant period is not exactly visible to the baby's watchful parent, I certainly found it an apt metaphor for that thrilling assumption of knowledge to which I found myself witness.

Not long after I first understood that she understood, Ella sat on her floor clutching her little blue C block, small enough to fit in the palm of her hand. Turning it over and over, she lighted on the picture of a cow, and began humming: "Mmmmmmm." I looked up from my book.

"Ella, what does the cow say?"

"Ah-mmmmmm."

"That's right," I said. "Mooo."

"MMM-mmmmmm," she hummed, her voice rising and falling, owning her own slight knowledge. She smiled and waved the block at me.

The moment frightened me a little because her learning was so quick and the moment of recognition so complete. I don't know exactly why this should have been the case, except that knowledge itself can be so startling. One day there is no language, no comprehension. Then something happens and there it is, a word flying out of the mouth like a butterfly broken from its chrysalis, a newly minted gift of a thing.

Over the next days she spoke "ra, ra, ra" for ruff, ruff, ruff, and "teh, teh, teh" as she pointed to her toes. I feared that I was not keeping up with her. Soon she would point or wave to every object in her range of vision. "Ahhh-ahhh-ahhh," she exclaimed, looking quizzically to me. "Table," I said. "Candle." "Plant." "No, no," I said and she shook her head in response. "Water . . . bath . . . fish . . . diaper . . . brown bear." Language tumbled through her at an alarming rate. By her first birthday she was able to pick out each of her books from her shelf, scan their spines like a little librarian until, Aha!—she recognized the title we had asked for.

Then, just two days after Easter, we visited the zoo with my parents. The children's area of the zoo was awash with toddlers, strollers, and small animals: miniature donkeys, ducks, sheep, goats, alpacas, hens, roosters. Most of these roamed free. We stood in front of a sheep. Ella stared intently as I petted its wooly coat. This was not her first time at the zoo.

"Do you want to pet the sheep?" my mother asked.

For a moment Ella watched me and then, to our astonishment, she shook her head. Back and forth deliberately it wagged. No.

My mother and I exchanged a look.

"Oh," I said.

Under her breath my mother exclaimed, "Hmm."

"Ask her again," I said.

"Would you like to pet the sheep Ella?"

Firmly, my daughter shook her head.

I laughed, not quite believing what I had seen. Thoughts clogged my brain. She had understood not only what was said, but that a question had been asked of her and it demanded a response. There were several levels of cognition at work, all of which seemed impossible to me.

It was not long before she could string together a sequence of ideas. Late one afternoon she crawled up to our front door, pulled herself to stand, and began to bang on it with the palm of her hand, banging and waving, banging and waving.

"Bye-bye," I said.

As if to acknowledge my correctness, she banged and waved with increased fervor.

"Bye-bye," I repeated. "Who went bye-bye?"

At this she stopped, turned around, and pointed to our wedding picture, which hung high on the wall behind her. "Dada," she said, and then she turned to me, a questioning look on her face.

"That's right," I exclaimed, "Dada went bye-bye to work. But he'll be home later."

"Bah-bah," she waved.

I understood that I would forever be in danger of underestimating her, that she would always be one step ahead of me. Now that she could think, her being was severed from my own: independent and just a little bit more unknown.

Watching Ella it seemed impossible not to believe that the brain is wired for language. How else to make sense of that sudden flash of understanding? There is a widely acknowledged theory of Universal Grammar, which helps to explain the mystery of language acquisition. Pioneered by linguist Noam Chomsky, the theory posits that because all language shares a fundamental underlying structure, the human brain must somehow be wired for language. Most languages are made up of similar parts of speech (noun, verb, object, adverb, etc.); all languages rely on a system of grammar (the particular order and construction of sentences). The universality of this system and structure suggest that language is unique to and inherent in the human mind. This is not to say that we know the rules of any particular language at birth, but rather that we are programmed to learn the rules as we confront them in our environment. How else to explain the ability of very young children to construct new sentences or to make plural forms of nouns or past tenses of verbs that they have never before heard? Certainly, children learn language by modeling adults, but they are also programmed to learn it; thus, their earliest efforts to communicate (the need for food, the desire to be held) are bounded and controlled by this innate propensity for deciphering and learning the human language that surrounds them.

Anyone who has listened long to baby's jargon understands intuitively this deep structure of language. For as soon as babies begin to notice the language around them, they begin to imitate. Their babble is nonsensical as "Jabberwocky" but equally suggestive of meaning. It rises and falls in pitch and tone and contains pauses and halts as if punctuated by commas, semi-colons, periods, or even question marks. All babies understand, eventually, that language is expressive, that phonemes strung together communicate desire, need, pleasure, or distress, and their babble erupts as if it does, indeed, have meaning. In fact, Ella's nonsensical speech was so often uttered with such deep insistence that it was impossible to think that it did not have meaning to her. Many days I nearly forgot she couldn't talk. Not only did I find it quite easy to understand her; it was easy to believe that she believed she made sense. Something deep in our make-up, something physical and irreducible, seemed to course through her, emphatically sentencing her to meaning.

Of all the things a child must learn, the most momentous is language. One day that undifferentiated stream of sound, of babble and bark and hum that flows from her mouth becomes intelligible. An insistent syllable or two frees itself from the crowd, its contours resolve, and a word becomes recognizable, a pattern that can be picked out of noisy chaos, or a clarion sound that becomes attached to meaning, to pedestrian sense. It is the most complicated and specialized knowledge of all. First she must hear, then recognize, then finally understand that the sound she hears, the symbol now round with meaning, offers her a new, illimitable map of her world. From that first Eureka! to the more nuanced understanding of verbs, commands, questions: *Go! Come! Put in your block! Take out your bunny!* is not so great a leap as that very first flight out of prelinguistic darkness. It is a flight that equals the greatness, if not the danger, of Satan's journey out of hell. It certainly brings her to knowledge most divine.

I remember the moment clearly, perhaps more clearly than any other of her first year. I had been working all day, sitting at the computer drafting and redrafting a new syllabus. I had hardly spoken to Ella, much less held or played with her. She seemed content playing with her father on the floor behind me. Suddenly she broke away from him and crawled over to me, plodding on all fours, her head down and wagging back and forth like a small animal. She stopped right below me. Then, with some effort, she balanced on her knees and pulled herself up on my chair. At full attention below me, she looked in my face and barked, "Ma!"

I looked down at her with equal parts shock and love. It was not her first word but it was her first real call for help. Her voice sounded foreign to me, as if language was not something I was ready to hear from her mouth, still largely the province of gutturals and labials.

"Ma!" she barked again, and I scooped her up into my arms. I did not know then that the Latin *infans* means "incapable of speech," but as I held her close I knew that it was the end of her babyhood.

Then I had my butterfly moment. I understood: all my life had been arcing toward this moment. I was not the same person I had been before. The transition had been radical and complete. Motherhood had made me someone new, but it had also returned me to myself. I would not say—I would emphatically not say—that motherhood completed me. I had never been conscious that something was missing. Yet in that most primitive word, in Ella's simplest monosyllable, I found myself collapse, disappear, and open up newly.

Whether it was fate or destiny or a more mysterious, chance-driven journey, I knew it as surely as I loved my daughter: my life could not have been otherwise. Out of nothing she had become something, and I had become something more. If the crushing love that I felt for her made me newly and forever fearful of mortality, and if, on some days, it made me tired and irritable and beside myself with despair and fury, there was something else, too, something with wings rising now like hope, or gratitude, or grace. I scooped Ella up in my arms and held her for a moment. Then I put her back down and returned to my work.

SELECTED
BIBLIOGRAPHY

Als, Heidelise. "Towards a Synactive Theory of Development: Promise for the Assessment of Infant Individuality." *Infant Mental Health Journal* 3, no. 4 (Winter 1982): 229–43.

American Academy of Pediatrics. *Your Baby's First Year.* Edited by Steven P. Shelov. New York: Bantam, 1998.

Beecher, Catharine E., and Harriet Beecher Stowe. *The American Woman's Home or, Principles of Domestic Science.* Edited by Nicole Tonkovich. New Brunswick NJ: Rutgers University Press, 2002.

Beecher, Henry K. "Pain in Men Wounded in Battle." *Annals of Surgery* 123, no. 1 (January 1946): 96–105.

Blackburn, Susan Tucker. *Maternal, Fetal, and Neonatal Physiology: A Clinical Perspective.* 3rd edition. St. Louis MO: Saunders, 2007.

Crittenden, Ann. *The Price of Motherhood: Why the Most Important Job in the World Is Still the Least Valued.* New York: Metropolitan Books/Henry Holt, 2001.

Eisenberg, Arlene, Heidi Murkoff, and Sandee E. Hathaway. *What to Expect When You're Expecting.* New York: Workman, 2002.

Eliot, Lise. *What's Going on in There? How the Brain and Mind Develop in the First Five Years of Life.* New York: Bantam Books, 1999.

Evans, Joel M. *The Whole Pregnancy Handbook: An Obstetrician's Guide to Integrating Conventional and Alternative Medicine Before, During, and After Pregnancy*. With Robin Aronson. New York: Gotham, 2005.

Flanagan, Caitlin. *To Hell with All That: Loving and Loathing Our Inner Housewife*. New York: Little, Brown, 2006.

——. "How Serfdom Saved the Women's Movement." *The Atlantic* (March 2004). http://www.theatlantic.com.

Gopnik, Alison, Andrew N. Meltzoff, and Patricia K. Kuhl. *The Scientist in the Crib: Minds, Brains, and How Children Learn*. New York: William Morrow, 1999.

Johnson, Robert V., ed. *Mayo Clinic Complete Book of Pregnancy and Baby's First Year*. New York: William Morrow, 1994.

Melzack, Ronald. "Pain: Past, Present, and Future." *Canadian Journal of Experimental Psychology* 47, no. 4 (1993): 615–29.

Melzack, Ronald, and Patrick D. Wall. "Pain Mechanisms: A New Theory." *Science* 150, no. 3699 (November 19, 1965): 971–79.

Nilsson, Lennart, and Lars Hamberger. *A Child Is Born*. Trans. Clare James. New York: Delacorte/Seymour Lawrence, 1990.

Niswander, Kenneth R. *Obstetrics: Essentials of Clinical Practice*. Boston: Little, Brown, 1976.

Weissbluth, Marc. *Healthy Sleep Habits, Happy Baby*. New York: Ballantine, 2005.

Wolf, Naomi. *(misconceptions): Truth, Lies, and the Unexpected on the Journey to Motherhood*. New York: Doubleday, 2001.

Vaughan, Christopher. *How Life Begins: The Science of Life in the Womb*. New York: Times/Random House, 1996.

Winners of the River Teeth Literary Nonfiction Prize

Five Shades of Shadow
Tracy Daugherty

The Untouched Minutes
Donald Morrill

Where the Trail Grows Faint:
A Year in the Life of
a Therapy Dog Team
Lynne Hugo

The World Before Mirrors
Joan Connor

House of Good Hope:
A Promise for a Broken City
Michael Downs

The Enders Hotel:
A Memoir
Brandon R. Schrand

An Inside Passage
Kurt Caswell

A Double Life:
Discovering Motherhood
Lisa Catherine Harper

To order or obtain more information
on these or other University
of Nebraska Press titles, visit www
.nebraskapress.unl.edu.